THE ABC'S OF CLASSROOM DISCIPLINE

By the authors:

THE ABC'S OF CLASSROOM DISCIPLINE
LIFE STYLE: Theory, Practice, and Research
LIFE STYLE: What It Is and How To Do It

THE ABC'S OF CLASSROOM DISCIPLINE

Leroy G. Baruth

University of South Carolina

Daniel G. Eckstein

Louisiana Tech University

Illustrated by
Pam Sink

KENDALL/HUNT PUBLISHING COMPANY
2460 Kerper Boulevard, Dubuque, Iowa 52001

Library of Congress Catalog Card Number: 76-26376

ISBN 0—8403—1587—2

Printed in the United States of America

401587 02

CONTENTS

PREFACE

This book resulted from an awareness of many educators concerning the need of more effective skills and techniques for establishing effective classroom discipline. An attempt has been made in this book to provide a *practical* approach to resolving many of the common classroom difficulties experienced by teachers.

The theoretical orientation of the book originated with Alfred Adler and Rudolf Dreikurs, and has been further articulated by the Alfred Adler Institute of Chicago and by such noted educators as Drs. Thomas Allen, Heinz and Rowena Ansbacher, Raymond Corsini, Don Dinkmeyer, Harold Mosak, Miriam and W.L. Pew, Robert Powers, Bernard Shulman, and Maneford Sonstegard. The authors gratefully acknowledge Drs. Oscar C. Christensen of Tucson, Arizona and Francis X. Walton of Columbia, South Carolina who have significantly influenced the philosophical approach advocated in this book.

Although many people have helped the dream of this programmed text become a reality, we would like to say a special "thank you" to the following helpful individuals: Pam Sink, "short subjects" artist; Anita Paczuski, Judy Eckstein proofreaders; and Kay Tolley, administrative coordinator.

Three individuals also contributed significantly to portions of the book's content itself: Brent Koyle on encouragement; Jane Lawther on classroom meetings; and Bill Wells on positive classroom behavior. We gratefully acknowledge their significant assistance. Here's a shiny red apple for you all.

Lee Baruth
Dan Eckstein

1

INTRODUCTION

In attempting to maximize educational effectiveness, many school teachers find themselves in a dilemma. On one hand they voice a concern for democratic classrooms, realizing that authoritarian methods infringe on students' rights. A vicious "negative" cycle is often perpetuated as teachers try to impose their will on students. Such teacher actions often result in student rebellions, prompting stricter teacher measures. But the other extreme, permissiveness, is similarly ineffective because it leads to anarchy, a "do-your-own thing" type of attitude.

Thomas Gordon (1974) has characterized the "authoritarianism vs. permissiveness" syndrome, as a "win-lose" struggle. In Method I, authoritarianism, the teacher is recognized for his/her expertise, knowledge, and experience. It is also a *power-based authority,* resulting from teachers being able to dispense certain things students need or want (rewards) and the teachers power to inflict discomfort or pain. In such a "teacher win—student lose" syndrome, the following methods serve as the typical coping mechanisms which students employ: rebelling, resisting, retaliating, lying, blaming others, cheating, bossing others, an obsession with winning, starting "under-ground" protests, submitting to authority, becoming an "apple-polisher," conforming, or totally dropping out of school.

Teachers can exert such power in the classroom only as long as the students are in a condition of want, need, desperation, helplessness, or dependency. Eventually students will no longer tolerate being placed in such an inferior position, resorting to the rebellious activities described above.

But in doing away with such strict authoritarian methods, many teachers have gone from one extreme to another—that of permissiveness. In Gordon's "Method II" the students win and the teacher loses. Teachers then become controlled and manipulated by students, with the following teacher coping mechanisms being observed: retaliation (giving hard exams or "pop-quizzes"), resigning, escaping, developing psychosomatic illnesses such as ulcers, "buttering up" students, conforming, or doing a minimal amount of work.

Various combinations of permissiveness and authoritarianism appear equally inept. Thus, a new system is needed—one where the needs of students *and* teachers are recognized and met. In such a system teachers can help stimulate children from within rather than relying on external pressures or threats.

The educational philosophy underlying this book was initially espoused by John Dewey, and was later modified by Alfred Adler and Rudolf Dreikurs, and such humanistic educators as William Glasser and Thomas Gordon. It is based upon alternative methods of achieving power and authority, methods which paradoxically give teachers more influence in their classrooms, not less. Such a system is built on a democratic concept which views people as being worthwhile. And, as Gordon notes, when teachers become skilled in using nonpower methods to achieve discipline and order, they find themselves using a new language when referring to discipline. The traditional language of power ("control," "direct," "punish," "threaten," "setting limits," "policing," "enforcing," "laying down the law," "being tough," "reprimanding," "scolding," "ordering," or "demanding,") is replaced by a new "problem solving" vocabulary (conflict resolution, influencing, confronting, collaboration, cooperation, joint decision making, working out contracts with students, obtaining mutual agreements, winning students over, or agreeing to disagree.)

The result of such innovative teaching approaches is that *neither* students nor teachers lose, while the educational process is enhanced for everyone. For example, through the use of classroom meetings teachers will find students discussing relevant issues and forming better relationships with them. Replacing power with a problem solving approach results in a better learning environment for everyone.

Our emphasis will be on practical classroom applications which have been supported by relevant theory practice and research. Although theoretical assumptions will be presented, our main goal is to provide practical application for classroom teachers. Additional readings and research findings are available from selected readings listed at the end of each chapter.

A programmed text approach has been implemented because of the advantage of immediate feedback, progression in small steps, active responding, and self-pacing. Typical chapters will have an introductory prose section, followed by various programmed materials. A crossword puzzle in the appendix is presented to aid the reader with a final "working knowledge" of the concepts presented in the text.

The philosophy underlying the workbook and the practical illustrations are meant to be relevant for elementary, middle or junior high, and high school teachers. Although teachers should be aware of the developmental psychosocial, biosocial, and vocational development tasks as illustrated in books such as Gazda's *Group Counseling: A Developmental Approach,* the basic human relationships between teachers and student remains the same in all age groups.

The theoretical orientation of the book originated with Alfred Adler and Rudolf Dreikurs, and has been articulated by numerous other individuals since then. It is based upon the belief that the child is a social being who is motivated to find a place at home, school, and in the world at large. All behavior is purposeful or goal-directed, indicating various ways and means each person has discovered to gain status and significance. When children feel worthwhile as individuals, their "social-interest" will be high, and they will find their place as useful, helpful members of society. However, low self-esteem and social interest typify "unproductive" socially "useless" methods of gaining a place in the community, resulting in cheating, vandalism, absenteeism, discipline problems, etc., for school systems.

An emergent democratic relationship based upon mutual trust, dignity, and respect of teachers and students is being stressed. Rewards and punishment become replaced by encouragement and natural and logical consequences.

Chapter 2 examines basic mistaken goals of children, with chapter 3 describing ways for teachers to recognize and deal with ineffective behaviors. Chapter 4 discusses the use of encouragement and consequences as a means of improving classroom atmosphere, while classroom meetings are the topic of chapter 5. Chapter 6 demonstrates ways to increase positive pupil behavior. Representative examples of elementary, middle, and high school conflicts are presented in chapter 7. Additional readings, charts, and a crossword puzzle are included in the appendix and bibliography.

2

UNDERSTANDING THE PURPOSES OF BEHAVIOR

Before a teacher can take the appropriate action when a child is misbehaving, the teacher must first determine the purpose or goal of the child's misbehavior. In this book, the four goals of misbehavior developed by Rudolph Dreikurs, will be used as a primary approach to understanding and classifying misbehavior. These four mistaken goals are: attention, power, revenge, and inadequacy.

Misbehavior can be generally defined as a departure from commonly accepted standards for classroom conduct and can be evidenced in almost every classroom. It is our contention that a misbehaving child is a *discouraged* child. Students can be actively disturbing by talking out of turn, fighting, throwing spitballs, pushing, and engaging in a number of other behaviors that would even challenge the imagination of Dr. Seuss. On the other hand, students can be involved in passive misbehavior such as failing to do assignments, refusing to respond when called upon, and generally not participating.

There are two basic ways to determine which of the four mistaken goals is being employed by the misbehaving child. The clues include *how the teacher feels* when the child misbehaves and *what the child does* when the teacher corrects him or her.

ATTENTION

If the child's mistaken goal is attention, the teacher will probably feel *annoyed.*

Michael, a fourth grader, taps his pencil on his desk. "It drives me crazy, and annoys the other students, too," reports his teacher.

Another way to determine if Michael's goal is attention is to watch his response when he's corrected. If his goal is attention, he will probably *stop,* at least for a little while. He has succeeded in getting the attention he wants and will not act out again until he again feels the need for additional attention.

POWER

If the child's mistaken goal is power, the teacher will probably feel *challenged, anger,* or in *conflict* with the child. Often a teacher will have an accompanying "He can't do that to me" attitude.

The teacher of Chris, a first grader, comments, "Chris has plenty of ability, yet in the last several weeks he has not completed one assignment. I allowed him to finish his papers at home and bring them back the next day. Soon I noticed that he was just sitting, not attempting to begin any work in class. He was winning the battle of being allowed to finish his work at home, and, of course, I felt he couldn't get away with it."

Another way to determine if Chris' goal is power is to watch his response when he's corrected. If his goal, indeed, is power, he will *continue* or even possibly *intensify* his misbehavior. If the teacher and Chris are in a struggle for power, neither will want the other to win.

REVENGE

When the child's mistaken goal is revenge, the teacher will usually feel *hurt.*

Bob's fifth grade teacher reports, "Bob is always beating up younger children on the playground. He's promised me that he will stop, but he keeps this up during almost every recess. I have a hunch that he does this because he knows I want him to stop. Even though he appears to be cooperative in class, I have the feeling that this is his way of getting even with me, that he can hurt bigger, older me by beating up smaller children."

To verify Bob's revenge goal, the teacher can also observe his reaction when he's corrected. If Bob feels hurt and wants to get even, his goal is probably revenge. Children who are physically abused at home often demonstrate the mistaken goal of revenge.

INADEQUACY

When the child's goal is inadequacy, the teacher will probably feel frustrated, discouraged or like *giving up.* The teacher may feel she's tried everything and that nothing works.

Ann's junior high English teacher writes, "Ann sits in the back of the room during class. She makes no attempt to participate and seems to have no friends. When I ask her why she hasn't completed an assignment, she replies, 'I don't know how to do this; I guess I'm just stupid.'

The teacher will probably feel sorry and not tend to correct or reprimand a child whose goal is inadequacy. The teacher, like the child, will feel helpless.

Based on what you have just read, *turn to page 9* *and see if you can correctly identify Paul's mistaken goal.*

SECTION I: SITUATION I

Paul, a fifth grader has an aversion to sitting, and often wanders around the classroom at will when he's expected to be seated and working. When his teacher asks that he be seated, he responds, "No," and under his breath, "you can't make me." Before he mumbles 'make' his teacher reacts with, "Oh, yes I can."

What is Paul's mistaken goal?

1. Attention (Turn to page 12)
2. Power (Turn to page 14)
3. Revenge (Turn to page 16)
4. Inadequacy (Turn to page 18)

What are you doing on this page? Can't you follow directions! Are you a nut or something? These are responses students (learners), such as yourself, have perhaps heard at one time or another.

You have not been directed to this page. The type of attitude we are trying to foster is one characterized by firmness and friendliness. So may we suggest that if you would like to profit from the programmed section of this book that you return to page 9 and read the directions.

You identified *attention* as Paul's mistaken goal. There are two clues to work with in this example: Paul's response to correction and the teacher's attitude or feeling. If Paul's goal is attention, he would have stopped the misbehavior and returned to his seat, for at least a little while. The second clue, the teacher's feeling or attitude, would seem to be much stronger than the feeling of annoyance which accompanies the attention provoking misbehavior.

Now that we have your attention, please return to page 9 and select another alternative.

LIST

Hurray! You correctly interpreted the clues like Sherlock Holmes. Paul's mistaken goal is power. The two identifying clues were Paul's continuation of his misbehavior when the teacher corrected him and also the fact that his teacher felt challenged and became involved in the struggle with her, "Oh, yes I can" reply.

Turn to page 19 for another situation.

You identified Paul's goal as *revenge.* If Paul's goal were revenge, he would have intensified his misbehavior when corrected, eliciting a hurt feeling from his teacher. In this situation, the teacher's "Oh, yes I can" response was like "throwing in the gauntlet," a challenge for combat.

Although we don't want to hurt your feelings, may we suggest that you return to page 9 and select another alternative.

NOTES

You identified *inadequacy* as Paul's mistaken goal. Paul's misbehavior, wandering around the classroom, and his "You can't make me" attitude eliminate inadequacy as a mistaken goal. If his goal were inadequacy, the teacher, like the child, would tend to feel helpless and ready to give up.

Don't give up. Please return to page 9 and select another alternative.

SITUATION II

Greg disturbs my entire class by playing, talking out, getting out of his seat, and, in general, interrupting activities. When Greg is reprimanded in class, he stops for awhile before embarking on some other misbehavior.

The first day I met Greg his mother told me he was hyperactive and on medication. I had observed how well Greg seemed to keep his mother in his service. Every other day she appeared with the lunchbox he'd left in the car or the homework he'd misplaced. I began to feel that he was attempting to do the same with me. I was annoyed because he was keeping me so busy and disrupting the class.

What is Greg's mistaken goal?

1. Attention (Turn to page 20)
2. Power (Turn to page 22)
3. Revenge (Turn to page 24)
4. Inadequacy (Turn to page 26)

You selected *attention* as Greg's mistaken goal. No doubt your choice was influenced by the fact that Greg would stop his misbehavior when reprimanded and also the annoyance his teacher felt when he disrupted the class. Your diagnosis is correct.

Turn to page 27 for another situation.

You chose *power* as Greg's mistaken goal. If his goal were power, he would intensify, or at least continue, his misbehavior when corrected and his teacher would feel challenged and overcome with a "Sit down because I told you to" feeling. In this situation, Greg discontinued his misbehavior for awhile when reprimanded and the teacher felt annoyed, not challenged.

Please concentrate your mental power on the clues and select another alternative on page 19.

NOTES

You concluded that *revenge* was Greg's mistaken goal. There are two clues on which to base your diagnosis: (1) the teacher felt annoyed by Greg's actions and (2) Greg stopped his misbehavior temporarily when reprimanded. If revenge were the mistaken goal, the teacher would feel hurt and Greg would engage in activities designed to get even with his teacher.

Follow the clues on page 19 to select another alternative.

NOTES

You selected *inadequacy* as Greg's mistaken goal. If Greg's goal were inadequacy, his teacher would feel like giving up, helpless. In this situation, however, the teacher feels annoyed. Normally, a student with the goal of inadequacy will be passive in his misbehavior, rather than very active as in this situation with Greg.

Don't despair. Flip back to page 19 where success in the choice of another alternative awaits.

SITUATION III

Mary chose to sit in the last desk in the row next to the wall. Except for an occasional comment, I wouldn't know she was in the class. When given a new assignment, Mary will usually just sit there, doing nothing, except, perhaps, writing her name on the top of her paper. When I ask her what's wrong, she usually replies, "I know I can't do it; I don't understand it," or "It's no use to try." I have tried several approaches in working with Mary with little or no success. I just don't know what more I can do.

What is Mary's mistaken goal?

1. Attention (Turn to page 28)
2. Power (Turn to page 30)
3. Revenge (Turn to page 32)
4. Inadequacy (Turn to page 34)

You selected *attention* which is a good guess. However, if attention were the goal of Mary's misbehavior, the teacher would probably feel annoyed. In this situation, the teacher's statement, "I just don't know what more I can do" suggests a feeling different from that of annoyance.

Please return to page 27 and select another alternative.

You selected *power* as Mary's mistaken goal. When the goal is power, the teacher usually feels challenged or has an ''I can make you complete that assignment'' attitude. In this situation, Mary's teacher appears to have made many efforts to help Mary learn; however, she has reached a point where she feels she's exhausted her resourcefulness. This feeling on the part of Mary's teacher suggests another goal.

Please return to page 27 and select another alternative.

You selected *revenge,* which could be a possibility. If Mary was refusing to do her work as a way of getting back at her teacher and the teacher felt hurt, revenge would be a good hypothesis. However, in this case the teacher seems to feel like giving up which is indicated by her statement, "I just don't know what more I can do."

Please return to page 27 and select another answer.

You selected *inadequacy* as Mary's mistaken goal. No doubt you were strongly influenced by the teacher's feelings of giving up and Mary's replies indicating it was no use to try because she couldn't succeed anyway. Your analysis is correct. Mary appears to be a very discouraged student and will need a lot of help to regain a healthy self-concept.

So far you have correctly identified the mistaken goals in three situations. If you would like to try one more example, turn to page 35; otherwise turn to page 44 where you will find a discussion of specific remedial actions to take to counteract misbehavior in the classroom.

SITUATION IV

The assistant principal told me that he had received reports from students and parents that Tom, a senior in my homeroom and history class, has been harassing and shoving around some younger, smaller boys. Tom is nineteen, physically well-developed, but a weak history student. It seems as if his abusive behavior increases on the days I reprimand him. At this point, I hesitate to correct him for fear of what he will do to others. I've even spent extra time working with him. I don't know why he does this to me.

What is Tom's mistaken goal?

1. Attention (Turn to page 36)
2. Power (Turn to page 38)
3. Revenge (Turn to page 40)
4. Inadequacy (Turn to page 42)

You selected *attention* as Tom's mistaken goal. In this situation, the teacher's attitude is revealed by the "I've even spent extra time working with him . . . look what he does to me" statement. The teacher feels hurt that despite her efforts Tom continues to harass the smaller, younger boys. If Tom's goal was attention, the teacher would feel annoyed rather than hurt and Tom would temporarily stop, rather than take out his hurt on other students.

Please return to page 35 and select another alternative.

NOTES

You selected *power* as the purpose of Tom's behavior. If the mistaken goal was power, the teacher would usually feel challenged and have an "I'll *make* Tom stop picking on younger students" attitude. In this situation, however, Tom's teacher seems to feel hurt. This is indicated by his teacher's statement, "I've even spent extra time working with him" with a "how can he do this to me" attitude. Also, if Tom's goal were power, he would probably continue or intensify his actions when reprimanded by the teacher instead of taking his hurt feelings out on other students.

We suggest you return to page 35 and select another alternative.

NOTES

You selected *revenge* as Tom's mistaken goal. We can see that Tom wants to get even when he is reprimanded by his teacher. Because he finds it difficult to directly "get back" at the teacher, he retaliates indirectly by picking on younger students. The teacher also indicates a hurt feeling by the "I've even given him extra help; why does he do this to me" attitude. You can chalk up another correct diagnosis. The mistaken goal in this situation is revenge.

Now that you have successfully identified the mistaken goal in four situations, you may be asking yourself, "So what?" Well, after the goal has been identified, there are specific remedial actions the teacher can take. These actions are explained in the next chapter. After a "raid the refrigerator" break, we will meet you on page 44. Here's a bouquet of flowers for your effort.

You selected *inadequacy* as the mistaken goal in this situation. You can see, however, that Tom is very active in his misbehavior. Normally, when the goal is inadequacy, the misbehavior will be passive in nature. It is possible that Tom may be frustrated by school work that is too difficult for him; however, the act of abusing younger boys and the feeling expressed by his teacher indicate a different goal.

Return to page 35 and select another alternative.

NOTES

3

DEVELOPING TECHNIQUES FOR RECTIFYING MISBEHAVIOR

Once the goal of misbehavior has been identified, the next step is to take appropriate action. This action will differ, depending upon the specific goal of the student's misbehavior. Additional information is presented in Appendix A on Mistaken Goals and Positive Behavior.

ATTENTION

Students who are involved in misbehavior for the sake of attention believe that they are important only when people are involved with them. It is natural to want some attention; however, it becomes a mistaken goal when the child demands attention at inappropriate times, e.g., when the teacher is helping another student and the attention-seeking child keeps interrupting.

One way to cope with the attention-getter is to *ignore* the misbehavior. Frequently the misbehavior will stop.

Another way of dealing with the attention-getter is to acknowledge the individual when (s)he is acting constructively. Because most children want to please, the child is likely to continue these positive activities, having had his or her appetite for attention satisfied.

A third way to handle the situation is to give the child a choice of two options. One option would be related to the misbehavior. For example, a student not sitting properly in a desk could be asked if he or she would prefer to sit properly or to have the chair removed until he or she decides to use it correctly.

POWER

The student involved in misbehavior for the purpose of demonstrating power usually feels important only when being the boss or when maneuvering and manipulating to get one's own way.

The important thing for the teacher to do is to avoid getting into a power struggle. Here are a few suggestions that might help:

1. Offer students choices that are realistic, e.g. "Would you like to sit properly in your chair or would you prefer to stand while eating your lunch?"
2. Utilize class meetings so that the students themselves can establish rules and consequences.
3. Gather the facts before making accusations.
4. Discuss misbehavior with a student at a neutral time, not during the heat of the conflict.
5. Phrase requests in a way that will minimize an opportunity for a power struggle. Instead of saying, "*I* want *you* to. . . .," the teacher could say, "Let *us*..." or "*We* need to..."
6. When you find yourself in a power struggle, withdraw, either physically or mentally. Without your involvement in the conflict, the situation will dissipate quickly.

REVENGE

The revengeful child feels hurt and wants to hurt others. Many times teachers will punish the revengeful child for the misbehavior. However, this only reinforces and confirms that others want to hurt him or her. The consequence is that such a person then wants to hurt others more to "get even," thus perpetuating the cycle by constantly reconfirming that life is an endless theme of being punished and of punishing.

It is important to remain friendly with this child even when (s)he exhibits the worst behavior. Certainly, one cannot be allowed to endanger other students; however, the individual can be restrained in a firm, friendly manner. The child should be made aware that at least you, the teacher, are understanding the hurt feelings. Sometimes teaming this child with one who is respected by other classmates for group work or for mutually beneficial tutoring can be helpful.

A word of caution: revengeful children often test those who show them kindness, usually by doing something hurtful just at the time the helper feels progress is being made in the relationship. It is especially important to remain friendly at this time, and not to affirm the child's mistaken notion that others merely hurt the person.

INADEQUACY

Inadequate children feel they cannot do anything as a result of repeated failure, pampering, or having things done for them. They have become so discouraged that they have stopped trying. The task for the teacher is to encourage such individuals to do something—anything. Assigning some tasks in the classroom which are unrelated to academic work may help. When such individuals do make a positive contribution, it should be acknowledged by the teacher with a smile, a wink, a hand on his shoulder, or a kind word.

With such children it is best not to wait until an assignment, painting, project or other task is completed, since they may become discouraged before ever finishing. Rather, the teacher should give encouragement during the process. It may take quite a while to change a child with inadequate feelings, so be patient and don't allow yourself to get discouraged.

It is our belief many teachers set such unrealistically high expectations for their own ability to help such inadequate-feeling children that they themselves frequently become discouraged and feel inadequate. Teachers are not going to instantly "undo" attitudes and behaviors which have taken many years to form. However, by sending "powerful invitations" of encouragement and by noting progressive improvement, both teacher and student can achieve a greater sense of self-worth.

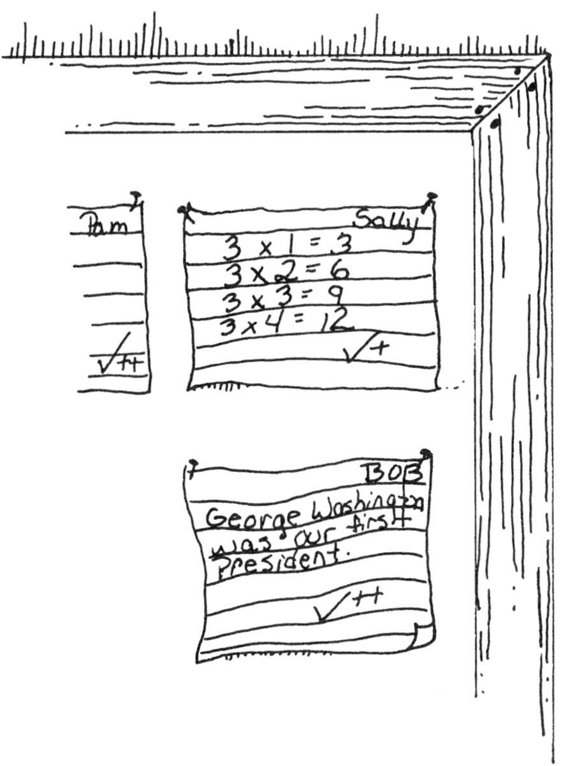

PREVENTATIVE—REMEDIAL TECHNIQUES

The use of class meetings and the practice of offering students choices are two techniques useful not only in coping with situations related to misbehavior in the classroom but also helpful in establishing a cooperative, democratic, friendly classroom environment.

A teacher can organize a class meeting into any format that (s)he feels comfortable in using. For example, the establishing of time daily or weekly in which the students can discuss class activities and problems, and the teaching of some basic principles of parliamentary procedure are helpful in promoting effective discussions.

Many times teachers feel that they bear the entire responsibility for classroom discipline. In reality, the class and the teacher working together are much more effective in preventing and coping with classroom problems than the teacher working alone. The attention-getter, the power-or revenge-oriented child, even the inadequate child, is more likely to change to more productive behavior when given the opportunity to have input to what is happening in the classroom. Children are more prone to have their behavior influenced by decisions made cooperatively with classmates.

Often the consequences of misbehavior are determined by the students in a class meeting, thereby removing the teacher from the role of judge and jury in the classroom. (Additional information on classroom meetings is found in chapter 5.) Allowing the misbehaving child a choice is a second important preventative-remedial technique. One alternative should be to stop the inappropriate behavior. The other alternative should be a statement of what the teacher is going to *do*, in form of a statement and not as a threat. The statement should never be one that cannot be implemented. For example:

Sam was constantly rocking on the back two legs of his chair. Based on a class decision, the teacher presented Sam with this choice, "Would you like to sit properly in your chair, or would you like me to remove your chair until you decide to sit properly?"

Frequently the child will stop the misbehavior when the teacher offers a choice. If, as in the case of Sam, the child continues to use the chair improperly, the teacher must follow through. It is important to give a child another chance, so the teacher may say something like, "When you decide that you would like to sit in your chair properly, I would be happy to bring it back to your desk," or "When you decide that you would like to sit in your chair properly, please be seated."

A friendly and cooperative manner by the teacher will help avoid getting into power struggles with students, as will encouraging the class as a whole to make decisions about classroom behavior.

HOW WOULD YOU HANDLE THESE SITUATIONS?

In your fourth grade class, Johnny constantly pokes the students sitting near him. His classmates and you get very annoyed with his behavior. When Johnny is corrected, he usually stops, but only for a short period of time. What would you do if Johnny were in your class?

1. Send Johnny to the principal's office. (Turn to page 50)
2. Tell Johnny, in the presence of his classmates, that his behavior is very annoying and selfish and that he should be ashamed of himself. (Turn to page 52)
3. Ignore Johnny's behavior as much as possible and figure out ways to channel his efforts to more constructive activities. (Turn to page 54)

PRINCIPAL

You elected to send Johnny to the principal's office. An advantage of this action is that Johnny will be out of the classroom, at least for a little while, and you and the other students will have some peace and quiet. However, if a child wants attention (Johnny's mistaken goal) badly enough, a trip to the principal's office is a small price to pay. Besides, all the commotion Johnny creates as he leaves the room to go to the office supplies him with an enormous amount of additional attention.

Please return to page 48 and select another course of action that might seem more appropriate.

NOTES

You elected to tell Johnny, in the presence of his classmates, that his behavior is very annoying and selfish and that he should be ashamed of himself. An advantage of this solution is that all the children in the class can learn what not to do. However, the effect this might have on Johnny's self concept is probably not worth the lesson gained by the other students. And, besides, if Johnny is really desperate for attention, he would be willing to accept negative attention and consider being shamed in front of the class a small price to pay.

Please return to page 48 and select another course of action that might seem more appropriate.

John

You decided to ignore Johnny's misbehavior as much as possible while figuring out ways to channel his efforts to more constructive activities. If Johnny really wants attention, he is going to get it.—As a teacher you are able to see that he gets it for positive behavior. If you ignore, or at least play down, Johnny's misbehavior and acknowledge his accomplishments (even though at first it might be difficult to identify positive behavior), he will soon realize that if he wants attention, it will be freely given for constructive, socially acceptable behavior.

Turn to page 55 and indicate how you plan to resolve the problem you are having with Susan.

An eighth grader in your English class refuses to do assigned classwork. Susan hands in a blank sheet of paper or a partially completed assignment and spends the rest of the time reading a library book. The "You can't get away with this" feeling is overcoming you, alerting you to a power struggle with Susan.

As Susan's teacher I would:

1. Arrange to have Susan stay after school and write one hundred times "I will do my classwork." (Turn to page 56)
2. Withdraw from the power struggle and try to win Susan's cooperation by capitalizing on her apparent interest in reading. (Turn to page 58)
3. Explain very politely that it is her responsibility to do her classwork and that you will keep her after school until she does it. (Turn to page 60)

You decided to keep Susan after school to write "I will do my classwork." This approach would most likely be a waste of paper and, at the same time, serve to add fuel to an already blazing power struggle between you and Susan. While writing, Susan would probably be telling herself something like, "You were able to win today by making me do this silly punishment. Wait until tomorrow in class; I'll show you who's boss!"

Please return to page 55 and select a more appropriate solution.

You opted to withdraw from the power struggle and to try to win Susan's cooperation by capitalizing on her apparent interest in reading. By removing yourself from the conflict with Susan, there can be no power struggle; it takes two to battle. Winning Susan's cooperation might be difficult at first, especially if the conflict over doing her work has been of high intensity and long duration. At first you would probably try to gain her cooperation by asking for assistance in a non-confrontive way. For example, you might say, "I could use some help in making this bulletin board for National Book Month; Susan, would you help me?" or, "Susan, would you help the class by reading the poem on page 50?" or "Susan, the librarian has asked that each English teacher have a student from each section work with her to update this suggested reading list; will you help me?"

After Susan's cooperation has been gained in some area, even if it's not directly related to the academic subject, it will be easier to resolve the classwork problem, if the problem hasn't already resolved itself in the process. However, if partially completed assignments continue to be handed in, make encouraging comments when appropriate, and do not stress the fact that they are incomplete.

Please turn to page 61 for a fresh conflict, a situation that has developed between Billy and John.

You said that you would politely explain to Susan that it's her responsibility to do her work and that you would keep her after school until she did it. You are right about the school work being Susan's responsibility; but it's difficult, if not impossible, to *make* anyone do anything! In addition to the inconvenience to you, keeping Susan after school will only serve to further alienate her and decrease your chances of gaining her cooperation.

Please return to page 55 to select another alternative.

Your sixth grade class has planned a unit on the Revolutionary War. The students were assigned to work in pairs on specific projects. Billy and John were in the process of reconstructing a model of the Battle of Yorktown when they began to argue as to which one of them was to glue the miniature plastic soldiers to the cardboard base. When the noise level became unreasonable, you went to investigate the cause. After hearing their story, you instructed John to glue the miniatures in place. As you turned away, Billy picked up the glue and poured some on John's head, saying, "I'll get even with you!"

As Billy's teacher I would:

1. Spank Billy and tell him never to do anything like that again. (Turn to page 62)
2. Send Billy to the principal's office and ask that his parents be called. (Turn to page 64)
3. In a calm voice tell Billy you would like to see him for a few minutes after class, excuse John to the restroom, and have the class continue their work. (Turn to page 66)

Your course of action would be to spank Billy and tell him never to do anything like that again. Chances are that spanking Billy would help you release the tension building up inside you; however, Billy would probably become only more enraged. He is feeling hurt and wants to get even. A spanking would most likely be interpreted by Billy as just another sign that people are unfair to him.

The authors vividly remember when male peers were "paddled" by either teachers or principals. At the first sound of a "whap," all conversation stopped while everyone counted the number of "licks" and noted whether or not the student cried. Although the paddling was generally followed with a stern lecture on the "evils" of such misbehavior, if the child received five or more strokes *without* crying, he returned to the class a hero.

Rather than feeling remorse, the child was often proud to have refrained from crying. The more strokes from the teacher or principal, the greater the praise from peers. Thus, the school officials were actually making misbehavior useful in that the student received much peer admiration and attention.

In your defense, it's only fair to mention that many teachers would be inclined to react likewise in this situation. However, there is another response that should be more helpful to Billy in the long run. Please return to page 61 to detect it.

NOTES

You elected to send Billy to the principal's office, asking that his parents be called. Billy's "I'll get even with you" statement indicates that his mistaken goal is revenge. Many teachers would follow the course of action you selected, believing that calling in outside help would resolve the situation, and it might for a short time. However, Billy is behaving the way he does because he feels hurt. Sending him to the principal and calling his parents will probably reinforce the feeling of hurt and increase the chance of similar incidents occurring in the future.

Please return to page 61 and select another course of action.

NOTES

You would try to remain calm and tell Billy you would like to see him for a few minutes after class. The fact that you are remaining calm and not over-reacting to the situation will help to reduce tension in the classroom. Talking to Billy after class instead of during the time of crisis will most likely be more productive than going into Sermonette #29 on Glue Pouring during a Revolutionary War lesson.

When discussing the situation with Billy, it is important to remain friendly, although the misbehavior should not be condoned. It would be appropriate to ask Billy what he believes should happen next (not what should have happened). Possibly he will suggest apologizing to John or, helping to clean up the mess. If his suggestions seem appropriate, allow him to determine what he will do next. If his suggestions seem inappropriate, you can either tell Billy what you intend to do or ask Billy to think about a course of action overnight and to explain it to you before class begins the next day.

A revengeful student is probably the most difficult to help. However, by remaining friendly, yet taking action, you will be progressing toward the elimination of Billy's feeling of hurt.

Your response is correct. Please turn to page 67.

Fred comes to your class almost every day; however, he sits in his desk very complacently, not participating in any class activities. Rarely does he complete an assignment although he doesn't disturb anyone. When you ask him why he doesn't do his work, he usually replies that it's too difficult for him. You've tried everything you know to encourage him, and you know that he has the ability to do the work, but thus far your efforts have been to no avail. You've reached the point of wanting to give up.

If you were Fred's teacher, would you:

1. Give him a task he can do, even if it's distributing papers or erasing the chalkboard? (Turn to page 68).
2. Display Fred's work on the board with other students' work so that he is able to see that he will have to work harder to do as well as his classmates? (Turn to page 70)
3. Ignore Fred because he will do the work when he feels he is ready? (Turn to page 72)

You indicated that you would give Fred some task that he could do, even if it was not directly related to academic work. It is important that Fred acquire a feeling of accomplishment. Once he has experienced success and received recognition for it, he will be more inclined to study.

With Fred it will be especially important to stress the positive. Don't dwell on the answer he missed, but emphasize the questions he answered correctly. You might consider marking items which are correct on his paper rather than incorrect items. You have selected the correct course of action.

Please turn to page 75.

NOTES

By displaying Fred's work on the board, you will show him that he is not doing as well as the other students. However, instead of encouraging Fred, this comparison may serve to discourage him even further. The important thing for Fred is that he do the best he can; whether his work is better or worse than his classmates is not the important issue.

Please return to page 67 and select another alternative.

NOTES

If we continue to ignore Fred until he feels ready to learn as you suggest, he may not overcome his feeling of inadequacy. He needs encouragement to try. The results of his efforts, no matter how small, should be given recognition.

Please don't get discouraged; return to page 67 and select another course of action.

NOTES

4

IMPROVING THE CLASSROOM ATMOSPHERE

In this chapter we will discuss three specific methods whereby teachers can improve their classroom environment. Through the use of encouragement, and by effective application of logical and natural consequences, teachers will enhance students' self-images while demonstrating that certain behaviors are not helpful in effective social interaction.

One of the most effective ways that a teacher can help students who consistently display the goal of inadequacy is through encouragement. Such acts instill in students feelings of confidence and prepare them for self-sufficiency. Encouragement should be contrasted with the all too frequent messages of discouragement which teachers communicate by humiliation, over-protection, and verbal assaults. Thomas Gordon (1974) has identified the following typical discouraging signals which teachers frequently send by what he terms the "twelve roadblocks to communication."

1. *Ordering, commanding, directing.* Example: "You stop complaining and get your work done."
2. *Warning, threatening.* Example: "You'd better get on the ball if you expect to get a good grade in this class."
3. *Moralizing, preaching, giving "shoulds" and "oughts."* Example: "You know it's your job to study when you come to school. You should leave your personal problems at home where they belong."
4. *Advising, offering solutions or suggestions.* Example: "The thing for you to do is to work out a better time schedule. Then you'll be able to get all your work done."
5. *Teaching, lecturing, giving logical arguments.* Example: "Let's look at the facts. You better remember there are only thirty-four more days of school to complete that assignment."
6. *Judging, criticizing, disagreeing, blaming.* Example: "You're just plain lazy or you're a big procrastinator."
7. *Name-calling, stereotyping, labeling.* Example: "You're acting like a fourth-grader, not like someone almost ready for high school."

8. *Interpreting, analyzing, diagnosing.* Example: "You're just trying to get out of doing that assignment."
9. *Praising, agreeing, giving positive evaluations.* Example: "You're really a very competent young man. I'm sure you'll figure how to get it done somehow."
10. *Reassuring, sympathizing, consoling, supporting.* Example: "You're not the only one who ever felt like this. I've felt that way about tough assignments, too. Besides, it won't seem hard when you get into it."
11. *Questioning, probing, interrogating, cross-examining.* Examples: "Do you think the assignment was too hard? How much time did you spend on it? Why did you wait so long to ask for help? How many hours have you put in on it?"
12. *Withdrawing, distracting, being sarcastic, humoring, diverting.* Examples: "Come on, let's talk about something more pleasant. Now isn't the time. Let's get back to our lesson. Seems like someone got up on the wrong side of the bed this morning."

Today, more than ever before, parents and professionals are conscious of the responsibilities involved in the area of child development. One part of this responsibility includes helping to provide for the child positive experiences which have a beneficial effect upon the whole being. Meeting this challenge often becomes difficult because our present social and educational systems seem to create an environment that sometimes leads to discouragement for the child. One aid available to assist in this challenge is for the parent or professional to know how to give genuine encouragement. To be able to effectively use encouragement is a very real skill. As in everything, it takes practice to develop these competencies. This chapter is an attempt to give some practical experience that will lead to the development of this skill.

Encouragement is not a single, unique event but it is a complex process that in the end will better help prepare the child for self-sufficiency. Dreikurs, *et al.* (1971, p. 65) explained this notion by saying that

> "teachers have a responsibility that goes beyond imparting facts and teaching skills. There is an even greater responsibility to reach each child and help him find a place in the group where he can find satisfaction and acceptance as a human being, regardless of how well or how poorly he performs scholastically. If the teacher succeeds in this endeavor, the child will most likely be able to respond to all learning situations in a positive receptive manner and progress toward developing true knowledge of the learning process. If she fails, he may assume too narrow limits for his capabilities and become a problem socially or scholastically, or both."

Before gaining the skill of providing encouragement, a parent, teacher, or other professional should conduct a self-examination. Determination should be made of what attitudes exist concerning children. Each child must be respected, on the premise of equality. Regardless of weaknesses and deficiencies children must be accepted *as they are.* Encouragement depends upon the attitudes and purposes of the person attempting to provide it. It is a process which communicates to the child trust, respect, and belief in oneself. Regardless of any lack of skills, the child's value as a person is never minimized.

In order to be encouraging we must first cease to discourage. Children who are discouraged are deprived of experiencing their own strength in testing how to overcome challenges and in learning to take care of themselves. Several common forms of discouragement include: overindulgence or over-protectiveness where children learn to depend on others and not on themselves; humiliation or punishment which often leads to a power struggle; and the use of comparison where children feel they never quite "measure up." Some children are given the feeling that they are important only if they are "better" than others. When a child fails to meet these imposed expectations (s)he feels defeated, resulting in discouraging self-perceptions. The proper use of encouragement will prevent the parent or professional from falling into one of these pitfalls.

The process of encouragement specifically involves:

1. Valuing individuals *as they are* not as their reputation indicates nor as you hope they will be—but as they are. Believing in individuals as good and worthwhile will facilitate acting toward them in this fashion.
2. Showing faith in the individual. This will help the individual to develop a feeling of "can-ness" or a belief in one's self.
3. Having faith in the child's ability. This enables the teacher to win the child's confidence while building the individual's self-respect.
4. Giving recognition for *effort* as well as a job well done.
5. Using the group to help the child develop. This makes practical use of the assumption that for social beings, the need to belong is basic.
6. Integrating the group so that the individual child can discover his or her place and begin working positively from that point.
7. Planning for success and assisting in the development of skills that are sequentially and psychologically paced.
8. Identifying and focusing on strengths and assets rather than mistakes.
9. Using the individual's interests in order to motivate instruction. (Dinkmeyer and Dreikurs, 1963).

Reimer (1967, pp. 72-73) lists ten "words of encouragement" which also helps to illustrate the encouragement process.

1. "You do a good job of. . ."
   Children should be encouraged when they do not expect it, when they are not asking for it. It is possible to point out some useful act or con-

tribution in each child. Even a comment about something small and insignificant to us, may have great importance to a child.

2. "You have improved in. . ."
   Growth and improvement is something we should expect from all children. They may not be where we would like them to be, but if there is progress, there is less chance for discouragement. Children will usually continue to try if they can see some improvement.
3. "We like (enjoy) you, but we don't like what you do." Children frequently feel disliked after having made a mistake or after misbehaving. A child should never think *he* or *she* is not liked. Rather, it is important to distinguish between the child and his or her behavior, between the act and the actor.
4. "You can help me (us, the others, etc.) by . . ." To feel useful and helpful is important to everyone. Children want to be helpful; we have only to give them the opportunity.
5. "Let's try it together." Children who think they have to do things perfectly are often afraid to attempt something new for fear of making a mistake or failing.
6. "So you made a mistake; now, what can you learn from your mistake." There is nothing that can be done about what has happened, but a person can always do something about the future. Mistakes can teach children a great deal, especially if they do not feel embarrassed for erring.
7. "You would like us to think you can't do it, but we think you can." This approach could be used when children say or convey the impression that something is too difficult for them and they hesitate to even try. An individual who tries and fails, has at least had the courage to try. Our expectations should be consistent with the child's ability and maturity.
8. "Keep trying. Don't give up." When a child is trying, but not meeting much success, a comment like this might be helpful.
9. "I'm sure you can straighten this out (solve this problem, etc.), but if you need any help, you know where you can find me."
   Adults need to express confidence that children are able and will resolve their own conflicts, if given a chance.
10. "I can understand how you feel (not sympathy, but empathy) but I'm sure you'll be able to handle it."

Sympathizing with another person seldom helps, rather it suggests that life has been unfair. Understanding the situation and believing in the child's ability to adjust to it is of much greater help.

Dreikurs, Grunwald, and Pepper (1971) provide thirteen additional ways for teachers to encourage their students:

1. If a child expresses doubt in his abilities in spite of the teacher's reassurance, (s)he may show reports of other teachers concerning him, if they are favorable. (S)he may say, "I don't do this very often, but I should like you to see for yourself that I am not the only one who believes in you. Listen to what Mrs. X said about you.
2. If a child is unsure and therefore does not start an assigned project, the teacher may sit down next to him and do part of the work with him. This may, in some cases, be enough to motivate him.
3. Let a child teach the entire class something he knows how to do well, no matter how insignificant it may be.
4. If the teacher senses that a child is unhappy because of his size—being too big or too small for his age, (s)he may read to the class about the achievements of great people who had the same problems. In this way, the child learns to evaluate himself and others not by size but by the person's personality.
5. Let a poor speller be the spelling teacher now and then, allowing him to use the book. The same may apply to any subject from which the child shies away.
6. Find special jobs for the child—jobs which give him status.
7. Let a child with poor writing habits write the teacher's assignments on the blackboard.
8. Ask a child who feels rejected to be master of ceremonies at a party.
9. Invite to speak to the class a member of the child's family who might make an impression on the others in class, if, for example, the child's father or brother is a policeman, fireman, or does work which is usually admired by children.
10. If the teacher knows of some special contribution a child makes at home, tell it to the entire class.
11. Display the child's work for everyone to see.
12. Invite the parents, and say in his presence something positive about the child to them.
13. Send a note home commenting favorably on the child's behavior, performance, or both. Teachers tend to send notes home only when children have difficulties.

Maintaining Sanity in the Classroom, Rudolf Dreikurs, Bernice Grunwald, and Floy Pepper, (New York: Harper & Row, 1971).

ENCOURAGEMENT VERSUS PRAISE

Teachers need to recognize the difference between praise and encouragement. For example, praise is usually given a child for doing a task well but encouragement is needed when the child fails. Encouragement during the actual task is as important as giving the child recognition at the completion of the task. Children once rewarded with praise may also interpret the absence of praise as signifying failure.

In an article entitled "Why Not Praise," Vicki Soltz (1967) notes the following:*

> How does praise affect the child's self-image? He may get the impression that his personal worth depends upon how he 'measures up' to the demands and values of others. 'If I am praised, my personal worth is high. If I am scolded, I am worthless.' When this child becomes an adult, his effectiveness, his ability to function, his capacity to cope with life's tasks will depend entirely upon his estimation of how he stands in the opinion of others. He will live constantly on an elevator—up and down.
>
> Praise is apt to center the attention of the child upon himself. 'How do I measure up?' rather than 'What does the situation need?' This gives rise to a fictive-goal of 'self-being-praised' instead of the reality-goal of 'what-can-I-do-to-help.'
>
> Another child may come to see praise as his right—as rightfully due him from life. Therefore, life is unfair if he doesn't receive praise for every effort. 'Poor me—no one appreciates me.' Or, he may feel he has no obligation to perform if no praise is forthcoming. 'What's in it for me? What will I get out of it? If no praise (reward) is forth-coming, why should I bother?'
>
> Praise can be terribly discouraging. If the child's effort fails to bring the expected praise, he may assume either that he isn't good enough or that what he has to offer isn't worth the effort and so give up.
>
> If a child has set exceedingly high standards for himself, praise may sound like mockery or scorn, especially when his efforts fail to measure up to his own standards. In such a child, praise only serves to increase his anger with himself and his resentment at others for not understanding his dilemma.
>
> In all our efforts to encourage children we must be alert to the child's response. The accent must move from 'What am I?' (good?) to 'How can I help the total situation?' Anything we do which reinforces a child's false image of himself is discouraging. Whatever we do that helps a child see that he is part of a functioning unit, that he can contribute, cooperate, participate within the total situation, is encouragement. We must learn to see that as he is, the child is good enough.
>
> Praise rewards the individual and tends to fasten his attention upon himself. Little satisfaction or self-fulfillment comes from this direction.
>
> Encouragement stimulates the effort and fastens attention upon one's capacity to join humanity and to become aware of interior strength and native capacity to cope.
>
> Praise recognizes the actor, encouragement acknowledges the act."

*Reprinted from *Study Group Leader's Manual,* Vicki Soltz (Chicago: Alfred Adler Institute, 1967) by permission of the publisher.

PRAISE	ENCOURAGEMENT
"Aren't you wonderful to be able to do this!	Isn't it nice that you can help?
I'm so proud of you for getting good grades. (You are high in my esteem.)	We appreciate your help. Don't the dishes shine? (after wiping)
I'm proud of you for behaving so nicely in the restaurant.	Isn't the carpet pretty now? (after vacuuming)
I'm awfully proud of your performance in the recital.	How nice your room looks!
	Thanks for watching the baby. It was a big help.
	I like your drawing. The colors are so pretty together.
	How much neater the room looks now that your toys are put away.
	How nice that you could figure that out for yourself. Your skill is growing!
	I'm so glad you enjoy learning (adding to your own resources).
	We all enjoyed being together in the restaurant.
	It is good to see that you enjoy playing. We all appreciate the job you did. I have to give you credit for working hard."

Using the notions previously discussed about encouragement; put a smiling face ☺ by the statements you feel are encouraging and a frowning face ☹ by those statements which could be discouraging.

1. We appreciate your help. You are so good at washing the dishes.
2. I'm awfully proud of your performance in the recital.
3. I like your picture. You have done such a nice job on these colors.
4. Why don't you work harder this term to get better grades.
5. I'm really having a problem. Would you help me work out a plan?
6. My, we had fun cleaning up the garage, didn't we?
7. I'm sorry you feel like that, but that is your privilege. You may think that if you like.
8. You sure did a nice job of mowing the grass.

If you had smiling faces for numbers 1, 3, 5, 7, 8 then you probably have a good understanding of the encouragement process. If you had some disagreement with the answers then the following reminders may help you to understand them:

- Emphasize the *deed*, not the doer.
- Emphasize the *doing* and the joy of doing. Satisfaction is gained in accomplishing something.
- Emphasize the *good part* of what was done.
- Be positive in comments made—avoid saying "don't."
- Avoid making statements ending with a question.
- Watch that a conditional acceptance is not communicated by building up on one breath and then deflating on the next.
- Give certain rights and privileges.

In each of the following statements write in what you consider would be an encouraging response for the circumstances:

A teacher has noticed that a student who has a very hard time with spelling has worked unusually hard all morning to improve his spelling . . .

Teacher's response: ____

____.

A normally well-behaved student for some reason is having a bad day. Twice she has been out of her seat and now you notice her disturbing a group of studnets working on a problem . . .

Teacher's response: ____

____.

Your son in eighth grade has brought his report card home. Most of the grades are in the B and C range; however, there is a D in English. How do you encourage your son in the area of English . . .

Parent's response: ____

____.

Check your responses to insure that they adhere to the principles previously discussed. Remember that the best way to integrate the skill of encouragement is through constant practice. In addition, there are a number of case studies enumerated beginning on page 87 of *Psychology in the Classroom* by Rudolf Dreikurs. Above all else it should be remembered that encouragement is a process which communicates to children respect and self-worth through accepting them *as they are.*

NATURAL AND LOGICAL CONSEQUENCES

Another method which teachers can use to stimulate children to proper and acceptable behavior is through the use of natural and logical consequences. *Natural consequences* represent the routine effects of reality or the natural flow of events without interference from parents or teachers. For example, the child who touches a hot stove gets burned. Children who do not eat soon get hungry. Natural consequences are imposed on children by the reality of the situation itself. The teacher can merely maintain the role of a friendly bystander.

Although natural consequences provide one of the most direct forms of learning, in many situations they are not realistic. For example, the natural consequence of playing in the street is for a child to get hit by a car. Naturally such a situation is undesirable; thus the need for logical consequences. *Logical consequences* are arranged or applied so that the consequence has an understandable relationship to the misdeed. In effect, they are arranged by the adult rather than being solely the result of the child's own acts.

Logical consequences involve a choice of behavior between two or more behaviors. For example, either the child or the parent may pick up the child's toys which are left in the living room. However, the person who picks up the toys has the option of what will be done with them. (The parent may decide to put them in the attic for a period of time). In the previous example where children are playing in the street, a logical consequence could be that they remain inside until they are able to play in the yard.

When natural and logical consequences are used, they should be understood and accepted by the child before their application. Consequences are also only effective if they are applied consistently. Such approaches can help prevent consequences from being viewed as another form of punishment. We define punishment as a method whereby "superior" teachers enforce their demands upon "inferior" students. Punishment is retaliatory, illogical, and arbitrary rather than corrective.

In *Logical Consequences: A New Approach to Discipline* Dreikurs and Grey (1968) chart the following important distinctions between consequences and punishment:

	Consequences	**Punishment**
1.	"Express the reality of the social order or the situation not of the person—Democratic	Expresses the power of a personal authority—Authoritarian
2.	Logically related to the misbehavior.	Not logical, only an arbitrary connection between misbehavior and consequences.
3.	Involves no element of moral judgement.	Inevitably involves some moral judgment.
4.	Concerned only with what will happen now.	Deals with the past.
5.	The relationship and atmosphere are friendly. Resentment is minimized.	Often anger is present either overtly or covertly. Resentment is frequent.
6.	Develop intrinsic motivation and self discipline.	Depends on extrinsic motivation.
7.	No submission or humiliation.	Often requires submission or humilitation.
8.	Freedom of choice within limits.	No alternative or choice.
9.	Consequences are acceptable.	Punishment is at best only tolerable.
10.	Thoughtful and deliberate.	Often impulsive.
11.	Child feels important.	Child feels belittled.
12.	Choice given once only.	Often involves endless nagging.
13.	Use Action.	Uses talking and coercion.
14.	The child accepts responsibility for his own actions.	The adult takes responsibility for the child's actions.
15.	The adult is disengaged from negative involvement with the child.	Involvement is always negative.
16.	Based on the concept of equality of worth between children and adults.	Based on superior-inferior-superior relationship between children and adults-fear of punishment.
17.	Implies that the child can work out his own problems.	Implies that only an adult is capable of solving the child's problems."

Using the principles of natural and logical consequences, put "NC" by the statements you feel are natural consequences, "LC" by situations which you feel employ logical consequences, and a "PU" by punishment oriented approaches.

___ 1. While playing with a frayed electric cord, Mary gets shocked.

___ 2. John habitually gets home from playing with his friends at 6:00 or 6:30 p.m. One day mother says, "supper is served at 5:30, if you get home after that, you can take responsibility for your own supper."

___ 3. After Sam brings home a "D" in math, his parents supervise his homework in math for a minimum of two hours a night.

___ 4. Because of constant fighting in class, Sal is required to stay after school and write "I will not fight" 200 times.

___ 5. Susan keeps leaving her toys in the driveway. One day her mother accidentally drives the car over her favorite model truck.

___ 6. Mother washes clothes on Wednesday—only clothing placed in the clothes hamper are included in the laundry.

___ 7. Johnny keeps fighting with students during class discussion. The teacher finally says, "Johnny, your fighting is disturbing the class; please move your chair to the other side of the room. However, when you are ready to join in our discussion, please come back into the group."

___ 8. The class is asked to stay inside and clean-up the art supplies prior to going outside to recess.

___ 9. Because Marsha is twenty minutes late for the "curfew" her parents have her "grounded"; she is not being permitted to date for two weeks.

___ 10. Students in home economics class are instructed to bring aprons from home to protect their regular clothing. Joan forgets to bring her apron, and the teacher reminds her that she will be unable to bake cookies that day as agreed upon in a previous classroom meeting.

Items 1 and 5 are examples of actions reflecting the natural consequence of an individual's action. Items number 2,6,7,8, and 10 illustrate a logical consequence between the individual's behavior and the action of the adult. Again it should be emphasized that logical consequences should not be imposed arbitrarily; such actions are also most effective if previously discussed with the child. Items number 3,4, and 9 are punishment techniques administered externally by a "superior" adult to an "inferior" child.

NOTES

5

CLASSROOM MEETINGS

One of the most effective means whereby a teacher can help students integrate educational curriculum into their daily lives is through the use of regular classroom meetings. In such sessions teachers are able to lead the class in non-judgmental discussions relating to what is important and relevant to the students.

In *Schools Without Failure,* William Glasser (1969) describes three different types of classroom meetings; the *social-problem-solving* meeting, the *open-ended* meeting, and the *educational-diagnostic* meeting.

The social-problem-solving meetings focus on individual and group problems of the class and the school. Such a problem-solving approach demonstrates that, although the world may be difficult and that at times it may appear to be hostile and dangerous, it is possible to use a creative individual and group problem-solving approach. Another benefit is that students are taught personal responsibility in controlling their own destiny. This contrasts with such less-desirable student behaviors as evading problems, depending upon others to solve their problems, or just "declaring bankruptcy" by not trying at all.

Social-problem-solving meetings typically focus on various behavior problems exhibited by students (i.e., fighting, cheating, disturbances). Other topics could include problems in such areas as friendship, loneliness, values, or vocational choices.

A second major type of classroom meeting identified by Glasser is the *open-ended meeting,* which he terms the "cornerstone of relevant education." In such meetings students are invited to discuss any thought-provoking question related to their lives, such as the curriculum of the classroom, or student relationships to one another and the teacher. The teacher's goal in such sessions should *not* be aimed at obtaining factual answers, but at trying to stimulate individuals to think instead.

The *Educational-Diagnostic Meeting* is always related directly to what the class is studying. It serves as a useful means whereby the teacher can get a quick evaluation of whether the curriculum can be practically applied to the daily lives of the students. Such meetings should concentrate on what

"working knowledge" students have regarding the class subject; they should not be used to grade or evaluate individual students.

In conducting an in-service workshop with teachers and administrators, William Glasser had the following educational-diagnostic type discussion with a group of eighth grade students who had studied the U.S. Constitution for a semester and a half. His classroom meeting sought to determine how much practical application the students had of their lengthy study of the constitution:

> My first question to the class was, "What is the Constitution?" The class seemed to be taken aback by this question, but I repeated it several times, adding, "I just want to know if anyone here can tell me what the Constitution is." Looking for some sort of definition or description to start the meeting, I saw immediately that the students were in trouble. It had never occurred to them that anyone would ever ask them what the Constitution is; assuming that everyone including themselves, knew, they hadn't bothered to think the idea through. The best answer I could get was that the Constitution is something written in books to be studied. I asked them, "Does the Constitution exist? Is there a Constitution on a piece of paper nailed to a wall somewhere that people can see?" The class doubted that it existed in the form I had described. Finally I had to tell them that the Constitution did exist and that people could go to Washington, D. C., and see it. (I usually don't give answers, but I was filled with frustration at this point.)
>
> From this small fractual start, I went on to see whether the students understood the ideas of the Constitution. Following their assurance that they had studied it in detail, I asked them to name some of its important features. When they mentioned the Bill of Rights, I said, "Do these rights pertain to you?" It took some time before they understood what I meant and more time to agree that in fact the Bill of Rights did pertain to the students sitting there. Some of them thought the Bill of Rights did pertain to them, while others thought that it was just for adults. To some extent the latter group was correct because, until the recent Supreme Court decision in the Gault case, minors had almost no protection under the law. Of course they had not learned this in their study of the Constitution.
>
> The key question, however, which brought on a discussion confirming my doubts about the students' understanding of the Constitution, was, "What happens if you do something on your own property that is against the law? For example, may you drive a car on your own property even though you don't have a driver's license and are too young to drive? May you drink a can of beer in your home if your father offers it to you, even though you are legally too young to drink?" I don't know the correct legal answers in these two examples, but that was not the point of the questioning. There was heated discussion. Many of the students suggested that you have no right to break the law on your own property and that you should be punished if you do. I then raised the question of how you could be caught. "Do the police have the right to spy on your house and then come in and arrest you if they think you are drinking beer with your father?" The class said they thought the police did have the right and should do so. I then asked them how the police would know whether a child was having a glass of beer with his father. Although they said that this would be hard to discover, they did have some constructive ideas. One of them was that the

police should have a television set focused in everybody's home and, as soon as the police saw anyone doing anything wrong, they should come and get him! Many in the class agreed with this idea and no one disagreed strongly. At that point we dropped the discussion.

It was clear that the discussion was provoking individual thinking about the Constitution. My affirmation of the existence of the Constitution in Washington was the only time during the discussion that I corrected the class or offered them a right answer.*

Listed below are several general principles for group discussions in classrooms:

1. An initial step in training children for group discussion is to talk about what is involved in a friendly discussion and to establish certain ground rules. For example, listen to others, stick to the subject, don't "clam up," and thinking together are excellent beginning guidelines. In groups of younger children it may be initially helpful to have children raise their hands when they want to speak.

2. All problems relative to the group or to individuals in the group should be eligible for discussion. Many teachers are reluctant to discuss various topics because of their own feelings of inadequacy involving certain topics. As adults, we need to be aware of our tendency to extend our own anxieties to children by modeling an evasive approach to difficulties. Also, it should be noted that it is *not* up to the teachers to solve the problems presented. Rather, (s)he should help the group focus on various alternatives to consider. But freeing teachers from sole responsibility for solutions, should encourage them to allow discussion of all problems.

3. As discussion leaders, teachers should encourage each child to contribute ideas. Quite often the verbal children will dominate the conversation, further alienating the shy, withdrawn class members. A teacher's invitation to such children could be, "we haven't heard from you yet, Johnny" or "what do you think about that idea, Suzan?"

4. The group discussion should always focus on solving the problems; the solution should never include punishment or fault-finding. Rather than focusing on what individuals are doing wrong, the purpose of the meetings is to help those who have problems to find better ways to live. The group should also realize that certain problems are not readily solvable, that there is seldom one single "perfect" solution, and that there may only be a "not-so-bad" alternative available.

5. When the teacher asks for possible solutions to various problems, student responses should be taken seriously. Teachers should refrain from contradicting or speaking critically of any child's offering. If teachers feel a

*From pp. 139-141 in *Schools Without Failure* by William Glasser. Copyright © 1969 by William Glasser, Inc. Reprinted by permission of Harper & Row, Publisher, Inc.

child is mistaken in his/her comments, they can ask the other children what they think of what was said, whether they agree or disagree, having them explain the reasons behind their beliefs.

6. Meeting duration should be based upon the age and group experience of the class. Primary-grade children find it difficult to maintain attention for more than 10 to 15 minutes. Eventually a discussion of 30 minutes can be effective, with meetings being held before recess, before lunch, or before the school's closing time. In upper-grades, discussions lasting 30 to 45 minutes have proven successful.

7. Meetings should always be conducted with the teacher and all students seated in a tight circle. Such an arrangement makes it possible for all children to see and hear, and it encourages better communication between group members.

8. Class meetings may occur spontaneously as needed, but a regular meeting time, a minimum of once a week, is also recommended. Teachers should realize that leading effective group discussions is a skill which improves with practice. Many teachers abandon class meetings due to initial frustrating experiences. Remember too, that the class needs to develop group discussion techniques. Most children are not used to having adults ask them their opinions, or to encourage them to identify and solve their own problems.

9. One particularly helpful method of beginning class discussion involves the teacher asking effective open-ended questions. Rather than only teaching "facts," such teachers are able to create vital discussion through the use of thought provoking questions. For example, consider some of the following questions:

"If you had enough money so that you didn't need to go to school to prepare to earn a living, what would you want to learn?"

"If your mother said you could stay home from school because it is a waste of time; would you be willing to stay home? If you did stay home, what things would you want to do?"

"Should your parents help you with your homework or should you do it by yourself?"

"What's the point in going to college? Must a person have a college degree to get a good job?"

"When you first came to school, how did you make a friend?"

"If you had the ability to change into an animal, what animal would you choose to become? What would you do as this animal?"

"If you were elected President of the U.S., what three things would you do?"

"If you had one million dollars to spend any way you wanted, how would you spend it?"

10. In classroom discussions, the leader should not incorporate value judgments into the discussion. Many teachers resist classroom discussions because value issues inevitably arise. Such adults often assert that the church and home should be involved in such discussions, with the school teaching children "facts" by means of a structured curriculum. It is our philosophy that schools should focus on "education for living" rather than just the traditional "three R's." Besides, we believe that it is impossible to remain value free in schools and that we only kid ourselves to believe otherwise. Thus, we assert that values are an important aspect of a child's education, and that students are aware of our values whether we consciously verbalize them or not.

However, we do want to distinguish between having a core set of values personally and expecting students to share the same set of values. As Simon, *et. al.* (1972), note, traditionally, adults motivated by a desire to have young people lead happy and productive lives, have guided them by moralizing ("My life has taught me certain values which I think will also be right for you"), by a "laissez-faire" approach ("no one value system is correct, so I'll just let my students find their own values by avoiding the topic") or by modeling ("I will live my life so that students will want to imitate me.") However, Simon advocates the values-clarification approach as a more desirable alternative. The values-clarification approach seeks to help young people answer pressing questions by building their own value system. It is based upon the approach formulated by Louis Raths, who in turn built upon the thinking of John Dewey. The *content* of people's values is less important than is the *process of valuing.* Raths (1966) believes that valuing is composed of seven sub-processes:

Prizing one's beliefs and behaviors

1. prizing and cherishing
2. publicly affirming, when appropriate

Choosing one's beliefs and behaviors

3. choosing from alternatives
4. choosing after consideration of consequences
5. choosing freely

Acting on one's beliefs

6. acting
7. acting with a pattern, consistency and repetition

Thus, the values-clarification approach does not aim to instill any particular set of values. Rather the goal of the values-clarification approach is to help students utilize the above seven processes of valuing in their own lives; to apply these valuing processes to already formed beliefs and behavior patterns and to those still emerging.

It is our belief that values clarification is a means whereby schools can avoid "teaching values" but, at the same time, can help students formulate their own beliefs and attitudes. We maintain that teachers often avoid classroom discussions for fear of such topics being discussed, and the possible repercussion of angry parents, etc. But, rather than avoiding or denying that we teachers do have values, we recommend the values-clarification approach in assisting students in prizing, choosing, affirming, and acting on their value system.

In *Teacher Effectiveness Training,* Thomas Gordon (1974) has an excellent chapter entitled, *"When Values Collide in School."* He encourages teachers to develop the following strategies in dealing with value collisions:

A. Become an Effective Consultant by observing four basic rules:
   1. He does not start out trying to change the student until he is certain *he has been hired.*
   2. He comes *adequately prepared* with facts, information, data.
   3. He shares his *expertise* succinctly, briefly, and only once—he doesn't hassle.
   4. He *leaves responsibility* with the student for accepting his efforts to effect change.

B. Model what you value.

C. Modify yourself to become more accepting. Suggested activities to become more accepting include: getting to know your students better, achieving personal growth through group or individual counseling, understanding your own values, and learning from students.

D. If there appears to be no way to reconcile basic value differences between you as a teacher and your students, then have the courage to "agree to disagree," in a mutually respectful manner. (We certainly do not advocate that teachers deny their value systems. Rather, we hope to instill more tolerance and student choice from a variety of crucial value decisions).

11. Classroom meetings should never be used to evaluate or grade the students.

12. Teachers can use stories as a basis for discussions in helping children to understand. For example, *Maintaining Sanity in The Classroom* (1971) has an excellent chapter containing sample stories as well as additional sources of information where other children's stories may be found. Two other innovative resources are the "DUSO" kit (Developing Understanding of Self and Others), and the "TAD" kit (Toward Affective Development), which are published by American Guidance Services. Both kits have a variety of activities including role-playing, puppets, story telling, discussion questions, etc. They are both designed for use in elementary grades 1-6.

Teachers can also work with counselors in providing additional group guidance and group counseling activities. For example, the use of role- playing, sociodrama, play therapy, unfinished stories, the creative use of art, and activity-interview counseling are described in Gazda's *Group Counseling: A Developmental Approach.* The book is also recommended because it utilizes various bio-socio-psychological tasks (Tryon and Liliental), psychosocial developmental tasks (Erikson), and vocational developmental tasks (Super) for each age group.

CLASSROOM MEETINGS: A PRACTICAL EXAMPLE

The following section describes an actual classroom discussion lasting six weeks. Group discussions can be open-ended (no set length or duration) or closed (a set time and number of sessions). In the example, it was decided that six meetings would be held once a week.

The teacher is initially active in helping establish the "ground rules" but subsequent discussions become student lead. An outline developed by Jane Lawther, a counselor at Pine Ridge (S.C.) Middle School, follows.

First Class Discussion

"We're going to be doing something new in home-room for a few weeks. Every *Thursday* we'll be having a class discussion. A class discussion is a special kind of time when we'll be thinking and talking together about how things are at our school and what we can do about them. Let's see the hands of those who would like to talk about how school goes."

"Class discussions or meetings are times for you as students to talk freely about things that give you trouble here at school. In the discussions we can work on our problems just as the teachers do in teachers' meetings. Some things we will be talking about are getting along with each other, getting along with teachers, listening to other people in a discussion. We'd like every person to share their ideas and opinions in the class discussions. How many would like to do this?"

"Before we start discussing we might need some ground rules. Let's see how these sound:

1. *Raising hands* to talk is a good way to take turns talking one at a time while others listen carefully.
2. *Comments* that hurt people are destructive and should not be used.
3. Since we have a short time, it is important to *stick to the subject.*

"What do you think of these ground rules? Are they fair? Do we (really) need other rules? How many will approve these rules?"

"O.K. let's begin. Let's have our first class discussion." Let's talk about homeroom time:

1. Who has an idea what homeroom is for? Why do we have homeroom?

2. What is good about homeroom? What do you like about it?
3. How could homeroom time be better? What suggestions would you make?

Second Class Discussion

Election of Student Representatives

"Today we're going to have our second class discussion. You remember that this is a time when we talk about living at school and how we can make things go better for ourselves at school. Last week we talked about some ground rules. Who can remember one of them? Another? We also talked about homeroom time and how things go in homeroom. What were some of the ideas that we talked about?"

"One of the things that we will learn in our class discussions is that it is useful to learn how to take responsibility. Today we as a homeroom are going to give some responsibility by electing some people to help our discussions."

"We will be electing three students to jobs that will help the group. One is the time watcher; one is a secretary; one is the agenda recorder. (1) the time

watcher will help us get started on time and give us a warning 5 minutes before homeroom time is over. (2) the secretary will write down the ideas that we talk about each time so that we can be reminded of what we have discussed. (An assistant may be a good idea.) (3) the agenda is a list of things to talk about to the agenda recorder, and we'll talk about as many as we can. The agenda recorder can check with the teacher if there is any question about the items on the agenda."

"Nominations are open for the election of time watcher." (A few names are gathered; students nominated are asked to leave the pod; a hand count is taken for the election.) The process is repeated for secretary and agenda recorder.

1. What are we telling people when we vote for them?
2. Why do you vote for people?
3. Is voting a good idea?
4. Is it better than having the teacher appoint someone? Why?
5. What does voting have to do with democracy?
6. How does it feel to be elected?

Assignment: "If you have anything you'd like to discuss in our class discussions, please give your ideas to Mary, our newly elected agenda recorder."

Third Class Discussion

Why We Go to School

"The first thing we'll be doing in our class discussions is to check with our agenda recorder to see what we'ss be discussing. Let's remember to stick to one topic since our time is short."

1. Mary, what suggestions do you have listed?
2. Which one shall we talk about first?
3. Who has an idea on the topic?
   (This question (number 4) is a good one to ask students who usually don't participate.)
4. How do you feel about that? About what another student said?

Alternate Plan: Why We Go To School (Adapted from Glasser, 1969)

1. Once when a teacher asked her students if their school work was related to their lives outside of school, they replied, "Of course not." What do you think of their answer?
2. If each of you could have a million dollars, would you go to school? Why?
3. If not, what would you do with your life?
4. Is what we are studying useful to us? Now? Later?
5. Do your parents think school is important? Why?

Fourth Class Discussion
Getting Into Trouble

1. Secretary, what did we talk about last time? Did we need to finish discussing anything?
2. Mary? What suggestions do you have for today's agenda?
3. Which one shall we discuss?
4. Who has an idea to share?
5. What do the rest of you think?
6. Think about a student leader for next time. Who could lead the discussion?

Alternate Plan: Getting Into Trouble

1. What happens to students at Pine Ridge when they get into trouble?
2. What should happen when students get into trouble?
3. Do students and teachers agree on what rules are important for school? Why? Why not?
   "I" questions for students to share their own feelings
   (Raths, Harmin, Simon, 1966)

1. My teacher doesn't like it when I . . . .
2. My teacher is easiest to get along with when I . . . .
3. Usually I get detention hall when I . . . .
4. What choices do I make that usually get me into trouble?

Fifth Class Discussion
Imagination Questions

1. Have you thought about a student leader? Should we elect or take volunteers? (Class makes the decision; a student may take over the asking of questions with the teacher participating.)
2. Secretary, what did we discuss last week? Was there anything else that we needed to discuss?
3. Agenda recorder, what do we have on our agenda for today?
4. Who has something to bring up?
5. How do the rest of you feel about that?

Alternate Plan: Imagination Questions (From Glasser, 1969)

1. Would you like to be the principal? The teacher? Why?
2. Would you like to be the superintendent of schools? Why? Why not?
3. If you were the principal, what would you do?
4. How would you treat the students in class if it were up to you to teach the class?
5. How would you treat the teacher if you were the principal?

6. If your teacher got sick and couldn't come to class, could you get along by yourselves if the principal could not find a substitute?
7. Do you think you could learn anything without a teacher?

Sixth Class Discussion
Unfinished Sentences

1. Who would like to be our student leader today?
2. Secretary, what did we discuss last week? Was there anything else that we needed to discuss?
3. Agenda recorder, what is on our agenda for today?
4. Who has something to bring up?
5. What do the rest of you think of that?

Alternate Plan: Unfinished Sentences (Simon, 1972)

1. People who agree with me make me feel . . .
2. People who disagree with me make me feel . . .
3. I get angry when . . .
4. I like best the kind of teacher who . . .
5. I like best the kind of friend who . . .
6. In school I do best when . . .
7. My teacher thinks I am . . .
8. I want most out of school . . .

This is the last one of our class discussions for now. How did you like them? Would you like to continue?

TEST YOUR KNOWLEDGE

As a summary of the chapter, answer the following questions.

A. Listing

1. List and briefly describe three types of classroom meetings as defined by William Glasser.
   a.
   b.
   c.
2. List eight (8) important principles for effective classroom discussion.
   a.
   b.
   c.
   d.
   e.
   f.
   g.
   h.
3. In the classroom discussion, what were the titles and functions of the three elected offices.
   a.
   b.
   c.

B. True-False

1. The purpose of an educational-diagnostic classroom meeting is to allow teachers to determine students ability to apply learnings in a practical manner.
2. All problems relevant to the group or to individuals in the group should be eligible for discussion in social-problem solving or open-ended meeting.
3. Value judgments are an important characteristic of the "values clarification" approach.
4. Classroom discussions are most effective when the usual seating arrangement by rows is maintained.
5. "My life has taught me certain values which I think will also be right for you" typifies the "laissez-faire" approach to values.
6. In the values clarification approach the *content* of people's values is more important than is the *process* of valuing.
7. In classroom discussions involving value decisions, teachers should not deny their own value system, but also allow tolerance of other opinions.

8. Classroom discussions are an excellent alternative means of student appraisal and grading.
9. Meeting duration should be based upon the age and group experience of the class.
10. The goal of discussion leaders in the classroom should be to help the class identify a "perfect" solution to their problems.

(Answers on page 131)

NOTES

6

FOSTERING POSITIVE PUPIL BEHAVIOR

Teacher: "Johnny, how many times must I ask you to pay attention to me: Now, turn around and face the front of the room."

Johnny turns around with an embarassed look and begins to sulk at his desk.

Teacher: "Now, we were talking about the time when President Lincoln went to the Ford Theater (teacher catches a movement out of the corner of her eye and turns to see Mary passing a note to Fred)...Mary bring me that note."

Mary: "It's nothing, Mrs. Turnipseed. I'll throw it away."

Teacher: "No!! Bring it here to me."

Mary: "Please, Mrs. Turnipseed, I'll throw it away and I won't do it anymore."

The previous dialogue could have taken place in many classes across the country. It happens so often it has become commonplace. Teachers respond as Mrs. Turnipseed did because they may not have had relevant instruction in how to deal with everyday problems in the classroom. As a matter of fact many teachers, particularly beginning teachers and teachers on the secondary level, leave the teaching field because of their inability to cope with behavioral problems in children (Eaton, Weathers and Phillips, 1957).

Sometimes the experienced teacher begins to slip into habits that allow behavioral problems to develop. He or she cannot understand why the children are becoming worse and presenting more problems every school year. Often such teachers are not aware that their own behavior is changing with each passing year which also causes the children to react differently to them each year.

At one time teachers used punishment to reduce or eliminate inappropriate behavior. Now, they realize punishment has negative side-effects (O'Leary and O'Leary, 1972). It was fashionable not very long ago for psychologists to suggest that "the classroom teacher is faced with two difficulties: identifying the behavioral problem child and obtaining, through referral, professional services for him" (Woody, 1969, p. 9). Thus, teachers came to understand they should refer all children who misbehave to a professional. They were warned that children might have serious physical, psychological or social problems that could only be solved by professionals. Later, school administrators told teachers they should not "discipline" children because they may be sued. This left the teacher in a roomful of children whom (s)he felt (s)he could not discipline and could not punish and had to refer to "professionals" if the children crossed their eyes. If the teacher referred all those who misbehaved (s)he would be in a room all alone while the "professional" would have all the children.

Well, the teacher is a professional too. The teacher has many behaviors he or she can use as first-aids for pupil misbehavior. This first-aid begins with some advance planning. The following are some suggestions for advance planning:

- Preview situations for possible danger or overstimulation (paints, gym, games or field trips) (Gnagey, 1965). Simply think ahead like a child.

- Write "reinforcement" notes home to parents (Hawkins and Sluyter, 1970). The teacher can have some general notes run off on a stencil machine for use such as: ____(name)____ has done exceptional work in ____(area)____ today. ____(name)____ work in this area is improving. Signed____(name and date). The teacher can then fill in the spaces as needed.

•Make curriculum a group activity as much as possible and "here and now." For example, when studying conservation assign brainstorming committees to produce questions, then assign committees to find answers. The teacher can help the children organize paper recycling in each child's neighborhood and have them write letters to newspapers and congressmen.

•Examine your curriculum and dispense with irrelevant academic exercises such as asking the children to write a letter to a senator when they have nothing to say. Letter writing can be worked into other curriculum—see above.

•Make a chart with each child's name and a folder for each child that holds his or her assignment for that day. This will allow the teacher to control for those who are faster than others.

While the above suggestions require advanced planning, the teacher may want to work on long-range relief from pupil misbehavior by changing or modifying some of his or her habits in the classroom. The following suggestions fall into the classification of general classroom habits:

•Greet each child at the door. This immediately develops a relationship between teacher and child.

•Keep class work moving with few or no slack periods. When the class keeps moving it makes time go quickly for teacher and students and allows little time for misbehavior to begin.

•For younger children, keep variety in their work. Younger children have shorter attention spans and, thus, require a more frequent change to another type of study.

•Provide a brief outline on the blackboard of the day's work and what is expected. This provides structure for the children and keeps them on task.

•Ignore small insignificant misbehavior (Gnagey, 1965). When teachers do not attend to insignificant misbehavior, the misbehaviors tend not to appear again because the child has not found them to be attention-getting behaviors.

•Recognize effort, not necessarily results. This refers back to encouragement, the topic of chapter 4.

•Plan a success for the child who has recently misbehaved. If a child has recently been a behavior problem, the teacher may want to ask a question the teacher is sure (s)he can answer. Or, the teacher may request help in some way. This has the effect of encouraging the child and bringing him or her back into the group.

•Embrace, pat, or hold the hand or arm or hold a well behaving child in the teacher's lap. Many teachers do just the opposite which encourages children to misbehave because then they are allowed to sit in the teacher's lap (Thomas, Becker and Armstrong, 1968).

•Post good work on the bulletin board (Krumboltz and Krumboltz, 1972). This provides reinforcement, encouragement and modeling for others as well as providing a specific example.

•Encourage each child in relation to his or her own prior performance, not in relation to the performance of others or the class as a whole.

•Be consistent in encouragement for all children, otherwise some may feel left out.

With good advance planning and good classroom habits like those suggested above, the teacher can manage to squelch most problems before they develop. There are times, however, when even the best laid plans of mice and men and teachers go astray. That is when the teacher needs a first-aid kit figuratively speaking. Below are some ingredients to be placed in every teacher's first-aid kit for pupil misbehavior:

•Move toward children without looking at or speaking to them (Gnagey, 1965). This will tend to remind the child to control himself.

•Use other children as models. When Johnny is turned around and speaking to Fred, the teacher might say, "Look at how nicely Marty is sitting in his seat and looking at me. I know you all can do as well." This calls the misbehaving child's attention, provides a model for appropriate behavior, calls attention to the specific behavior requested, and does not call attention to the inappropriate behavior demonstrated by Johnny.

•Encourage the misbehaving child. To Ferdinand who is sitting at his desk and not coloring as requested, the teacher might say, "Ferdinand, I know you can color well and I will be looking forward to seeing what an interesting picture you will have for me."

•Gently touch the child. This is a little more than simply moving toward the child. By touching the student the teacher may remind him that the teacher is near and is supportive of the child. Touch is also a non-verbal way of reassuring.

•Call the child's attention back to his or her work. This focuses on what the child is supposed to be doing; not on what (s)he is doing wrong. It also provides clues for specific behavior, and can be encouraging because it implies that the student can do the work.

•Send signals such as a finger to the lips, shaking the head or a glance (Gnagey, 1965).

•Reflect the misbehavior's feelings. When a child comes into the room mad at another, the teacher can begin a classroom scene by telling the child to be quiet and sit down. The teacher may, instead, simply recognize the child's

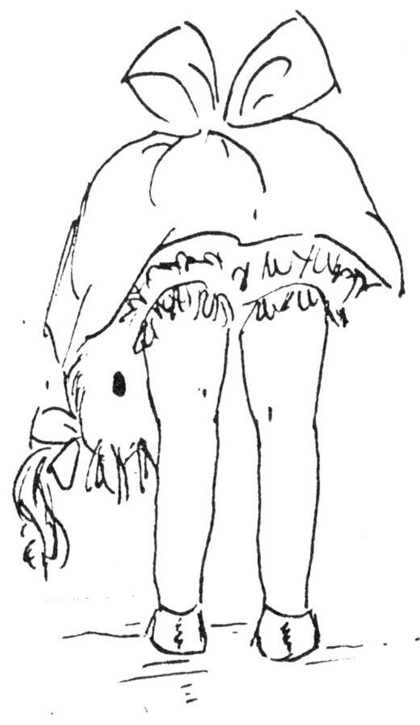

feelings by saying, "You're really mad at Ralph." Such an attitude reflects empathetic feelings and a basic sensitivity toward the student.

•Give the misbehaver the benefit of the doubt. Say, "You were probably busy getting your math book out, James, so I will give the math assignment again." This is much better than, "I'm not going to say it again because you weren't listening."

•Give assistance. Do not make the child say (s)he does not know an answer when it is obvious (s)he does not know. When the child stammers or responds to a question with a long "Uhhh," the teacher may want to suggest the child can find the answer and then ask another student to answer the question.

•Removal of the child to another part of the room or to another room. The teacher may choose to put a student in a remote part of the classroom or in another room when the student indicates he is having difficulty. Such a brief "time out" period should also provide an opportunity for the child to return to the class when (s)he can behave.

•Show faith in the child. When a student misbehaves, the teacher cannot erase the behavior the child has displayed, but the teacher can do something to keep it from recurring. The teacher can point out to the student that the behavior is inappropriate but that the student is accepted as an individual. The teacher can encourage the student to behave more appropriately the next time.

Helping students realize positive attributes should be an ongoing goal for teachers. Weekly "self-affirmation" sessions where pairs of students have two minutes each to share "what I appreciate about me is ____________, my strengths are ____________, or I am improving at ____________ "have proven highly successful. A final two minute sharing can focus on "strengths I see in you." Many teachers have also used "appreciation envelopes," (similar to "valentine containers") with each student's name on the outside. Students are then encouraged to write positive comments of appreciation on slips of paper and "deposit" them in the individuals "appreciation envelope." Teachers can minimize the "I got the most valentines" syndrome by encouraging students to write sincere positive comments for all classmates. The notes may or may not be signed by the student but class time should be used for individuals to publicly affirm their strengths.

Naturally, there are many more things teachers can do. There may also be physical, psychological or social circumstances that produce misbehavior in the child. The teacher should be professional enough to recognize that when misbehavior continually reoccurs, then the child needs to be referred to another professional.

NOTES

7

SOLVING CLASSROOM SITUATIONS

The format of this chapter is designed to allow you to solve real classroom problems. More than twenty situations have been selected from actual teaching experiences with public school students to provoke your responses. The problems are presented on one page and space for you to write your solution is provided on the opposite page. On a separate page there will be a suggested solution based on information presented in earlier chapters of this book. Please note that there are many possible solutions to each of the problems presented and the solutions listed are only suggestions. It is also quite possible that some of these suggested solutions might be inappropriate for your particular school setting. However, the important point is for you to utilize the principles studied in a manner that would be acceptable for your classroom.

Now please turn to the situations that are appropriate for your teaching level. If you are an elementary school teacher, see page 111, middle school teachers turn to page 113, and high school teachers turn to page 115.

Write in how you would solve each of the situations. Good luck.

ELEMENTARY SCHOOL SITUATIONS

1. One of your first grade students had not completed a single assignment in the first three weeks of school. When you mentioned this, the little girl just smiles and does nothing. You would:
2. You find one of your second graders has taken another student's paper, erased his name and placed his own name on it. You would:
3. Two students continually fight in the classroom. Nothing makes them stop. However, when separated they laugh and say they were just playing. You would:
4. A first grade child refuses to get out of the car when his mother brings him to school. The mother states that when this has happened in the past she would take him to the day care center where she works. You would:
5. After recess one of your third graders shows you a piece of paper with four letter words on it that he found on the playground. He wants to know what they mean. You would:
6. Steven asks to go to the bathroom every class period. After he is told no, he persists in talking or beating on the desk in order to receive permission. You would:
7. You are supervising a playground during recess. You see two first grade girls who are best friends, argue and then begin to fight. You would:

YOUR SOLUTION

1.

2.

3.

4.

5.

6.

7.

(see p. 117 for suggested solutions)

MIDDLE SCHOOL SITUATIONS

1. In your seventh grade class Mary says Jane has her red and blue pen. You have seen Mary with the pen before. Jane says she brought the pen from home. Mary insists Jane took her pen and wants you to have Jane give it to her. You would:
2. You are a fifth grade science teacher. You went to the office on business between classes. When you get back to your room a white boy and a black student are the center of attention. From what others in the class say as you walk in, you assume there has been race-related name calling. The whole class is in chaos. The two boys seem to be hot under the collar and about to fight. You would:
3. You reach an eighth grade math class. While taking a test you see Mary copying David's paper. You would:
4. While you are on bus duty, several sixth grade boys are throwing footballs in a restricted area. One boy throws the ball on top of the building. You would:
5. When you briefly step out of the classroom, two fifth grade boys start fighting. When you return the other students are in a circle encouraging the boys to continue the fight. You would:
6. Two girls are talking in the back of the room and not paying attention. You are trying to conduct a reading lesson. You would:
7. You are teaching a spelling lesson to a fifth grade class. Jane screams out, disrupting the class, as an unsightly, huge spider crawls in front of her desk. The whole class is in an uproar now. You would:

YOUR SOLUTION

1.

2.

3.

4.

5.

6.

7.

(see p. 119 for suggested solutions)

HIGH SCHOOL SITUATIONS

1. Randy, a ninth grader, did well in math at first then suddenly quit working. He did not cooperate in class and refused to work. Most of the time he sits and draws but when he does listen, he talks constantly, repeating your words, answering out of turn, and talking back to other students. You would:
2. Tim, a high school junior, would often respond in a class discussion with comments concerning sex. Sometimes the other students would laugh. It appeared that Tim wanted to shock either his peers or you with his near-obscene remarks. You would:
3. Brad, an eleventh grader, has been disrupting class by talking and cutting up. You have had to ask Brad to leave the class when you felt you could no longer control his behavior. On occasion he is belligerent and combative. You would:
4. Curtis comes to class before all of the students, but he spends this extra time standing around your desk until you notice him. Once class has begun, he interrupts the normal routine by telling you personal things about himself or asking you personal things about yourself. If you listen to him or answer his questions, he is quiet for a little while longer. He does very little classwork, however, and he never bothers classmates except with this occasional discourse on himself or you. You would:
5. Tom, a senior, has been picking on freshman boys. He is nineteen and physically well-developed. The ninth graders are taking a beating and demand that something be done with Tom. You would:
6. You are teaching a tenth grade English class. It's "Book Report Day." When you call on John he's unprepared and has no excuse for his negligence. You would:
7. During a lunch period outside, you see a student pick up a 10-inch iron bar, put it under his jacket, and enter the school building. You would:

YOUR SOLUTION

1.

2.

3.

4.

5.

6.

7.

(see p. 121 for suggested solutions)

SUGGESTED SOLUTIONS FOR ELEMENTARY SCHOOL SITUATIONS

1. Give her a job that you are ninety nine percent sure she can do. Examples might be to pass out papers, be a line leader, or take messages to other classrooms. When these tasks are accomplished, she should be given recognition in front of the class. This girl feels very discouraged and needs to experience success even if it involves nonacademic tasks. As she gains confidence she will be more likely to attempt school assignments. When she does, effort and improvement should be recognized.
2. In a friendly but firm manner tell the student who handed in the wrong paper that you will accept his paper when it is complete. Then return the paper to its rightful owner. When the student does turn in his own work make every effort to use encouragement. A possible reason for the paper switching may have been a feeling of inadequacy.
3. When the two students are fighting you might give them the choice "would you like to do your school work now or during recess?" Possibly the first day they may elect to do the work during recess; however, subsequently students will usually choose to do the work when it is supposed to be done. Another possibility would be to follow a suggestion of Dreikurs and "put them all in the same boat." You would tell the class it is too noisy to teach so you will wait until everyone is quiet. You may elect to write the amount of time wasted on the chalk board and the class can make-up the time later.
4. This child has been able to get his way by not getting out of the car. The teacher might recommend that mother give the child a choice "you may get out of the car by yourself or I will help you." It is important that this choice be given in a friendly, but firm manner. The assumption is being made that the child must get out of the car and go to school. If the child doesn't answer, you could say, "I see you would like me to help you," and in a firm manner help him from the car. After a few mornings, if mother is consistent, the child will realize there is nothing to gain by staying in the car and will get out willingly.
5. Before you answer the question you may want to ask the child what he thinks the word means. If you are convinced that he is serious and not just playing a game, you might want to answer on a level he would understand. If you feel uncomfortable about answering the question you may want to refer him to another member of school personnel such as the school nurse. It is important if you decide to answer the question to answer directly and with as little answer as the question demands.

The story about the child who asked, ''Where did Mary (the next door neighbor) come from,'' is a good example. After a lengthy answer dating back to preconception the child says to the mother, ''Oh, I thought she came from Toledo.''

6. This would be a situation where a class meeting might be helpful. Many classes decide to have bathroom passes. When a child is out of the room the rest of the class will have to wait until he returns before they may go to the bathroom. This approach would remove the teacher from the position of deciding who can go to the bathroom and when. If the child continues to use the bathroom an excessive number times, even after the pay off (undue attention), has been removed the teacher might suggest that the child have a physical examination.
7. Your first action might be to let the girls work out the problem for themselves. If they continue to fight, you might make a comment such as ''If we can't play together, we will have to end recess.'' If the fighting pursists, do not give another choice, but just announce recess is over. You could end recess just for the two girls involved, or use the ''all in the same boat'' and take the whole class back to their room. If fighting is a common problem, it should be discussed at a class meeting.

SUGGESTED SOLUTIONS FOR MIDDLE SCHOOL SITUATIONS

1. The tendency for many teachers in this situation would be to play referee and try to decide who is the real owner of the pen. Usually this approach takes a lot of the teacher's time and fosters student dependency on the teacher. A possible solution would be for the teacher to take the pen and tell the girls to decide who the owner is and then she will be happy to return the pen. This gets the teacher out of the almost impossible task of deciding who is right and it also shows faith that the two girls can resolve the situation themselves.
2. With the situation at a near explosion point you would want to defuse it as fast as possible. This could be done by asking the two boys involved to step outside the door and discuss the situation. When the pressure from the peer group to fight is removed, the situation may start to equalize. Get the rest of the class involved in some type of school work, and then step outside to see if the two students have cooled off. When their tempers have cooled they can return to class. If race relations are usually this volatile, class meetings should be used to head off such confrontations.
3. When you see Mary copying David's paper you could ask her to come up to your desk. Tell her that you would not give her a grade on the test because it reflected David's work. You would also want to determine the appropriate mistaken goal. Many times cheating stems from a feeling of inadequacy. Basically the student is saying "I don't think my work is good enough, so I'll copy someone else's." If this is the case, it is important for the teacher to use frequent encouragement to help Mary gain confidence in herself. Possibly Mary could even help the teacher grade papers!
4. When the boys approach you about their problem you can sympathize with them but you should not let them get the football. They were playing in a restricted area and a risk is that the football might land some place out of reach. A consequence would be to just leave the ball on top of the roof or if someone does remove it (such as a custodian) to deny the boys the further use of it until they can play in the proper place. If they promise to use it outside of the restricted area, you can let them try again. However, if it is used again in the restricted area, you will confiscate the football.
5. The situations with fighting usually involve an audience. You should first ask the students who are fighting to leave the room and then get the other students working. Many times when students are denied an audience they will not find it reinforcing to fight. If fighting is a fre-

quent problem, you would want to discuss the situation and possible consequences during a class meeting. You would also want to find ways for the two boys to work together possibly on a joint project. This idea would be discussed with them at a later time and not at the moment of conflict.

6. With the two girls not paying attention, one possibility might be to use modeling behavior. A statement directed at a student who is paying attention such as "Alice, you are doing a good job of participating" many times will temporarily correct the misbehavior. You might also want to see if you could get the two girls actively involved. Or, if the girls talk constantly, you may wish to have a conference with them and explain that they may continue to sit together as long as they don't disturb the class. Then if they talk at inappropriate times, separate them. Another possibility would be the "all in the same boat technique." When the girls start talking, stop teaching. Note on the chalk board the amount of time wasted and the class can make-up that time later, such as recess or after school. The teacher will not have to say much because the peers will usually keep the two girls quiet in the future.
7. You or a student in the class could catch the spider and keep it for science class. Thank Jane for finding the spider and continue with the spelling lesson. Unexpected interruptions such as this occur frequently during the school year. Situations should be acknowledged, and class continued as soon as possible.

SUGGESTED SOLUTIONS FOR HIGH SCHOOL SITUATIONS

1. The fact that Randy did well in math indicates he has the ability. You might want to have a conference with him and discuss possible problems he might be having (home, girl friend, etc.). You might also ask him if he would be willing to help a student having trouble with math. Peer teaching would be a way of getting Randy involved in constructive behavior. If a student's goal is attention, the teacher should channel the student into activities where attention can be given for constructive, rather than destructive behavior.
2. Tim will probably continue to make comments concerning sex as long as he is being reinforced by the reactions of you and his peers. You might want to ignore his remarks and also encourage other students to do the same. Ignoring is only a temporary step, however, it is important that Tim does get the attention he needs. The teacher should get him involved in positive activities that will gain the attention of the other students. When Tim realizes his need is being met by his new behaviors, there will be less need to continue his misbehavior.
3. Be careful to avoid getting involved in a power struggle with Brad. Be on the lookout for anything that you can compliment. Solicit his help with some classroom jobs such as: passing out papers, working on bulletin boards, and taking messages to other classrooms. Admit that Brad has power. Mention that there are really few things you can make him do. Try to get him to cooperate with you because he wants to, not because he feels you are trying to force him to do so.
4. Curtis is displaying the symptoms of attention with a little "puppy love" thrown in. Because he has the strong desire for your attention you can give him recognition only when he is doing his school work and ignore his behavior when he is being nonproductive. He will soon learn that if he wants your attention, it will have to be gained through constructive behavior.
5. The fact that Tom is spending so much time with the younger students may be an indication that he is not being accepted by his own peer group. You should explain to Tom that his behavior cannot continue and then the two of you might discuss appropriate consequences. The most important point to remember however, is that punishment will probably not help the situation. A positive approach must be used to let Tom know that he is OK—the way he is. And he doesn't have to try to prove it by beating up on students who are physically inferior.
6. When John doesn't have his report ready, go on to the next student without making any comment to John. At the end of the class period

ask John if he knows the consequence of not having his work completed on time. If the class has not previously established consequences for not completing work on time, you should ask them to do so at the next class meeting. You might also want to explain that it is his responsibility to finish his work and if he doesn't accept this responsibility, he will experience the consequences of his actions. It is important, also to make positive comments when John does submit his work. This will encourage him to continue with his school work.

7. Obviously you can't allow a student to have a weapon such as a 10 inch iron bar in school. You, and possibly another teacher, might want to confront the student by saying "as you know, dangerous weapons are not allowed in school—would you like to take the iron bar back outside or would you like me to." Usually, the student will remove the bar, but if this is not the case, *do not* try to take the iron bar from him. Immediately report the situation to school officials.

APPENDIX A

Recognizing Mistaken Goals and Instilling Positive Behavior

As Carlson & Faiber (1976) note, all behavior has a purpose or is directed toward the achievement of a goal. Children as well as adults have needs—the most important of these being the sense of belonging and the feeling of significance or importance, whether it be in the family, the peer group, or the community. In order to find our place in life, we will behave (or misbehave) in ways to achieve these goals. Because all behavior is goal-directed, a transaction that involves two or more samples of behavior by an individual will reflect movement toward the goal. Therefore, by using the "ABC System" of understanding human behavior developed by Don Dinkmeyer and Jon Carlson (1973), it is possible to accurately identify the goal in a short period of time. This procedure involves

A—Observing what the child or person does

B—Identifying what the reactor (parent or teacher) does and how he/she feels

C—Recording the consequences of the transaction or how the person responds to (B)

After observing several situations, a pattern in the behavior will emerge and the goal or purpose of the person's behavior can be seen.

In the socioteleological or Adlerian approach to understanding human behavior, (Adler, 1957; Dreikurs, 1950), it is thought that children misbehave to reach one of four basic goals.

Goal 1. *Attention.* The child believes "I am important only when people notice me or are in my service" or "I'm not outstanding but at *least* I will not be overlooked if I can obtain special attention, fuss, or service."

Goal 2. *Power.* "I count in life when people do just what I want" or "I may not be a winner but *at least* I can show people they cannot defeat me or stop me from doing what I want or make me do what they want."

Goal 3. *Revenge.* The discouraged child who seeks this goal believes "I count or I'm special only when I hurt" or "people do not care for me, but *at least* I can do things to strike back when I am hurt."

Goal 4. *Inadequacy.* The child who seeks this goal has given up on life and feels "I do not count, why bother?" or "I will not be able to measure up but *at least* if I do nothing, people will leave me alone."

Figure 1 uses the ABC System as a framework to identify the four goals of misbehavior. The understanding and facilitation of healthy or productive behavior can be seen in Figure 2. Once an individual's goal and purposes are discovered, then appropriate modification plans can be developed. It is important to stress that modification programs have three fundamental aspects: (1) removing unwanted and inappropriate goals and their corresponding behavior, (2) encouraging and developing already existing goals and behavior and, (3) initiating new behavioral responses and healthy goals. Most people concentrate on eliminating existing behaviors, yet developing appropriate goals and responses will yield greater gains.

GOAL OF MISBEHAVIOR	"A" What the Child Does	"B" What the Teacher/Parent Do and How They Feel	"C" What the Child Does as the Consequence	What the Child Is Saying	Some Corrective Measures
ATTENTION	Active and passive activities that may appear constructive, destructive	Annoyed; wants to remind, coax; delighted with "good" child	Temporarily stops, disturbing action when given attention	"I only count when I am being noticed or served."	—Ignore —Answer or do the unexpected —Give attention at pleasant times
POWER	Active and passive activities only destructive in nature	Provoked, angry; generally wants power challenged —"I'll make him do it." "You can't get away with it."	Intensifies action when reprimanded; child wants to win, be boss	"I only count when I am dominating, when you do what I want you to."	—Extricate self —Act, not talk —Be friendly —Establish equality —Redirect child's efforts into constructive channels
REVENGE	More severe active and passive activities	Hurt, mad—"How could he do this to me?"	Wants to get even make self disliked; intensifies action in a hurtful fashion	"I can't be liked, I don't have power, but I'll count if I can hurt others as I feel hurt by life."	—Extricate self —Win child —Maintain order with minimum restraint —Avoid retaliations —Take time and effort to help child
INADEQUACY	Passive activities that defy involvement.	Despair—"I give up."	No reprimand, therefore, no reactions. Feels there is no use to try; passive	"I can't do anything right, so I won't try to do anything at all; I am no good."	—Encouragement (may take long) —Faith in child's ability

Figure 1. ABC System.

Reprinted from *Focus on Guidance*, Jon Carlson and Brenda Rifkin Faiber (Denver, Co: Love Publishing Company, 1976) by permission of the publisher.

Child's Belief	Goal	Behavior	How to Encourage Positive Behavior
I belong by contributing.	Attention Involvement Contribution	Helps Volunteers	Let child know the contribution counts and that you appreciate it.
I can decide and be responsible for my behavior.	Power Autonomy Responsibility for own behavior	Shows self-discipline Does own work Is resourceful	Encourage child's decision making. Let child experience both positive and negative outcomes. Express confidence in the child.
I am interested in cooperating.	Justice Fairness	Return kindness for hurt Ignores belittling comments	Let child know you appreciate his interest in cooperating.
I can decide to withdraw from conflict.	Withdrawal from conflict Refusal to fight Acceptance of others' opinions	Ignores provocations Withdraws from power contest to decide own behavior	Recognize child's effort to act maturely.

Figure 2. Goals of Positive Behavior.

Reprinted from *Systematic Training for Effective Parenting,* Don Dinkmeyer and George McKay (Circle Pines, MN: American Guidance Services, 1976) by permission of the publisher.

APPENDIX B

Classroom Management Puzzle

Across

3 Vehicle for communication exchange in classroom

4 Handle similar situations in a uniform way

5 Subtle behavior

7 Goal where reprimand will result in desire to get even

8 Not to be used to intimidate students

9 Possibilities to be considered

13 Working together toward common goals

14 Behavior is goal-directed

17 Goal where reprimand temporarily corrects the situation

20 Technique for disengaging from struggle

22 Hints for identifying mistaken goals

24 Feeling that stimulates person to retaliate

26 Accentuate this kind of behavior

28 Should be directed toward deed and not the doer

29 Goal where a reprimand is usually not given

Down

1 Basic technique used to cope with inappropriate behavior

2 Permitting the student to select an alternate behavior

3 Departure from commonly accepted standards for classroom conduct

6 Easily observable behavior

10 Used to reinforce attempts at appropriate behavior

11 Being accountable for one's actions

12 What student experiences as a result of a decision

15 More effective than talking in conflict situation

16 Irritation felt by teacher

18 Handle situation impartially

19 Goal where reprimanding intensifies conflict

21 Feeling of wanting to give up

23 Maintain this attitude even in times of crisis

25 Not being swayed by student protest

27 Ways to have others give in

(ANSWERS ON PAGE 132)

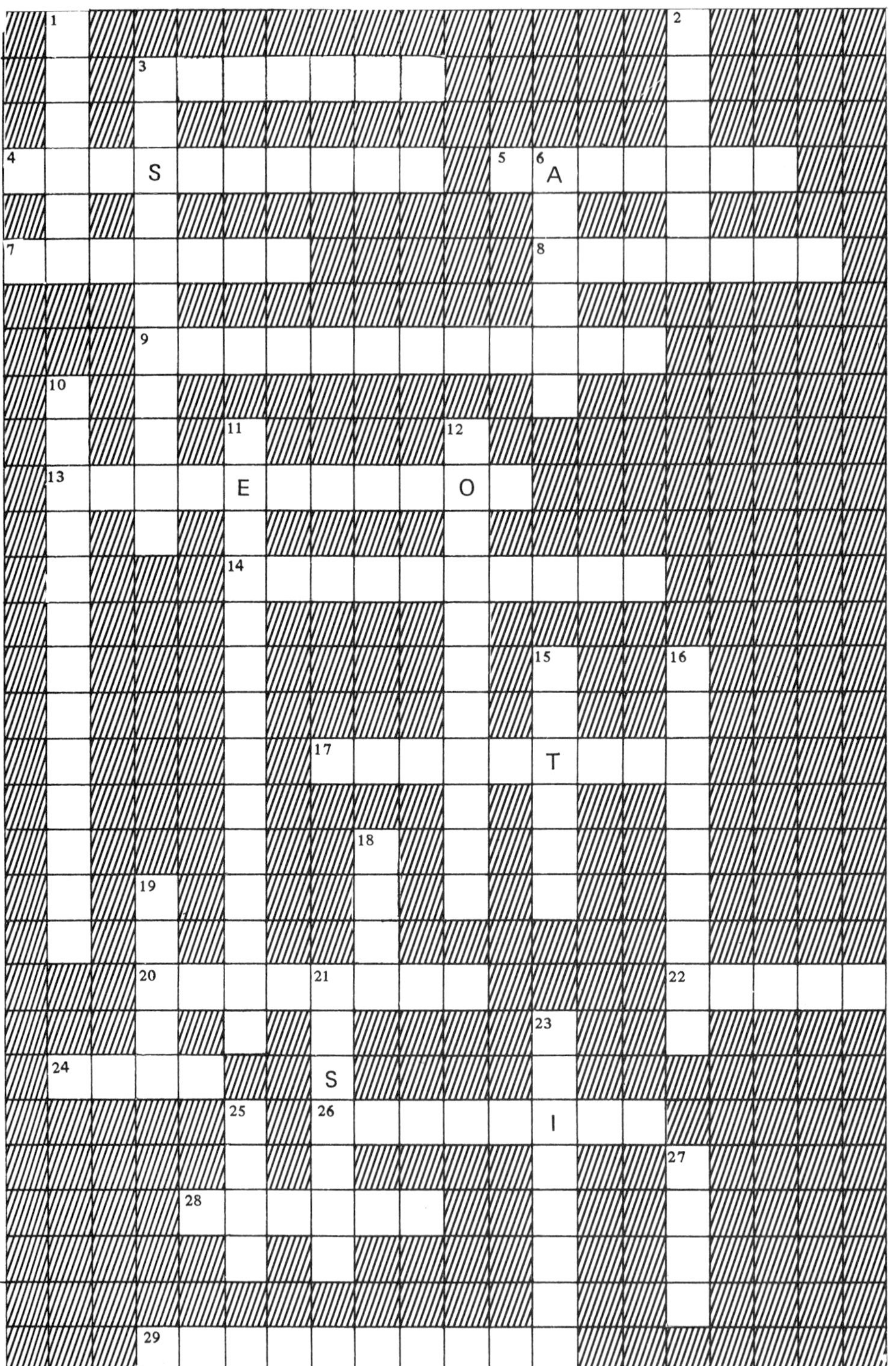
1
2
3
4
S
5
6
A
7
8
9
10
11
12
13
E
O
14
15
16
17
T
18
19
20
21
22
23
24
S
25
26
I
27
28
29

ANSWERS

A.

1.
   a. Social-problem solving (see page 87)
   b. Open-ended (see page 87)
   c. Educational-diagnostic (see pages 87-88)
2. See pages 90-94
3.
   a. Time keeper
   b. Secretary
   c. Agenda recorder (see pages 95-96)

B.

1. True (p. 87-83)
2. True (p. 90)
3. False (p. 92-93)
4. False (p. 91)
5. False (p. 92)
6. False (p. 92)
7. True (p. 92-93)
8. False (p. 93)
9. True (p. 91)
10. False (p. 90)

	1 I														2 C				
	G		3 M	E	E	T	I	N	G						H				
	N		I												O				
4 C	O	N	S	I	S	T	E	N	T		5 P	6 A	S	S	I	V	E		
	R		B									C			C				
7 R	E	V	E	N	G	E						8 T	H	R	E	A	T	S	
			H									I							
			9 A	L	T	E	R	N	A	T	I	V	E	S					
	10 E		V									E							
	N		I		11 R					12 C									
	13 C	O	O	P	E	R	A	T	I	O	N								
	O		R		S					N									
	U				14 P	U	R	P	O	S	E	F	U	L					
	R				O					E									
	A				N					Q		15 A			16 A				
	G				S					U		C			N				
	E				I		17 A	T	T	E	N	T	I	O	N				
	M				B					N		I			O				
	E				I			18 F		C		O			Y				
	N		19 P		L			A		E		N			A				
	T		O		I			I							N				
			20 W	I	T	H	21 D	R	A	W					22 C	L	U	E	S
			E		Y		E					23 F			E				
	24 H	U	R	T			S					R							
					25 F		26 P	O	S	I	T	I	V	E					
					I		A					E			27 B				
				28 P	R	A	I	S	E			N			O				
					M		R					D			S				
												L			S				
			29 I	N	A	D	E	Q	U	A	C	Y							

BIBLIOGRAPHY

Adler, Alfred. *Understanding Human Behavior*, New York: Faucett, 1957.

Baruth, Leroy & Eckstein, Daniel. *Life Style: Theory, Practice and Research.* Dubuque, Iowa: Kendall/Hunt, 1978.

Borden, Barbara. "Children's Discussion Groups: A Positive Force in Behavioral Change." *The Individual Psychologist,* 1978, 15 (1), 53-61.

Carlson, Jon, & Faiber, Brenda. "Necessary Skills for Parenting," *Focus on Guidance,* 1976, 8 (7), 2-3.

Corsini, Raymond. " 'Individual Education' Theme Issue," *Journal of Individual Psychology,* 1977, 33, 2a, 292-410.

Dinkmeyer, D. & Dreikurs, R. *Encouraging Children to Learn: The Encouragement Process.* Englewood Cliffs, New Jersey: Prentice-Hall, 1963.

Dinkmeyer, D. & Carlson, J. *Consulting: Facilitating Human Potential and Change Processes.* Columbus Ohio: Charles E. Merrill Publishing Company, 1973.

Dinkmeyer, Don. *Developing Understanding of Self & Others,* Circle Pines, MN: American Guidance Service, Inc., 1973.

Dinkmeyer, D., & McKay, G. *Systematic Training for Effective Parenting.* Circle Pines, MN: American Guidance Services, 1976.

Dreikurs, R. *Fundamentals of Adlerian Psychology.* New York: Greenberg, 1950.

Dreikurs, R., & Grey, L. *Logical Consequences: A New Approach to Discipline.* Hawthorn, 1968.

Dreikurs, R. *Psychology in the Classroom.* New York: Harper & Row, 1968.

Dreikurs, Rudolf; Grunwald, Bernice; & Pepper, Floy. *Maintaining Sanity in the Classroom,* New York: Harper & Row, 1971.

Dupont, Henry, *et. al. Toward Affective Development,* Circle Pines, MN: American Guidance Service, Inc., 1974.

Eaton, M.T., Weather, G. and Phillips, B.N. Some reactions of classroom teachers to problem behavior in school. *Educational Administration* and Supervision, 1957, *43,* 129-139.

Eckstein, D., Baruth, L., & Mahrer, D. *Life Style: What It Is and How To Do It.* Dubuque, Iowa: Kendall/Hunt, 1978.

Gazda, George. Group Counseling: *A Developmental Approach.* Boston: Allyn & Bacon, 1971.

Glasser, William. *Schools Without Failure,* New York: Harper & Row, 1969.

Gnagey, W.J. *Controlling Classroom Misbehavior.* Washington, DC: National Education Association, 1965.

Gordon, Thomas. *Teacher Effectiveness Training,* New York: Peter Wyden, 1974.

Greer, Mary & Rubinstein, Bonnie. *Will the Real Teacher Please Stand Up?* Pacific Palisades, Calif.: Goodyear, 1972.

Hawkins, R.P. & Sluyter, D.J. Modification of achievement by a simple technique involving parents and teachers. Paper presented at American Educational Research Association convention in Minneapolis, March 1970.

Krumboltz, J.D. and Krumboltz, H.B. *Changing Children's Behavior.* Englewood Cliffs, NJ: Prentice-Hall, 1972.

O'Connell, W.E. & Bright, M.D. *Natural High Primer.* Chicago: Alfred Adler Institute, 1977.

O'Leary, K.D. and O'Leary, S.G. *Classroom Management: The Successful Use of Behavior Modification.* New York: Pergamon Press, 1972.

Raths, Louis, *et.al. Values & Teaching,* Columbus, OH: Charles E. Merrill, 1966.

Reimer, C. "Some Words of Encouragement." In *Study Group Leader's Manual,* edited by Vicki Soltz, pp. 71-73. Chicago: Alfred Adler Institute, 1967.

Schlachter, Bartholomew, "Adolescent Group Counseling," *The Individual Psychologist,* 1978, 15 (2), 34-40

Seese, JoAnn. "How to Develop Social Interest Through A Class Council." *The Individual Psychologist,* 1978, 15 (1), 27-35.

Simon, Sidney; Howe, Leland; Kirschenbaum, Howard. *Values Clarification,* New York: Hart Publishing Co, 1972.

Soltz, V. *Study Group Leader's Manual* Chicago: Alfred Adler Institute, 1967.

Thomas, D. R., Becker, W.C. and Armstrong, M. Production and elimination of disruptive classroom behavior by systematically varying teacher's behavior. *Journal of Applied Behavior Analysis,* 1968, *1,* 35-45.

Woody, R.H. *Behavioral Problem Children in the Schools.* New York: Appleton-Century-Crofts, 1969.

Other Recommended Stories for Effective Group Discussions Include:

Andersen, H.C. *The Emperor's New Clothes.* New York: Oxford University Press, 1945.

Andersen, H.C. *The Princess on the Pea.* New York: Oxford University Press, 1955.

——— *The Ugly Duckling.* New York: Oxford University Press, 1955.

"Articles of Supplementary Reading for Teachers & Counselors," Chicago: Alfred Adler Institute, 1970.

Berghoff, C. *Where is Daddy?* Englewood Cliffs, NJ: Prentice-Hall, 1969.

Bollinger, Max. *Joseph.* New York: Delacorte Press, 1967.

Bullard, Maurice L. *The Use of Stories for Self-Understanding.* Maurice L. Bullard, 333 N. 6th St., Corvallis, OR, 1963.

Curren, Polly. "Whizzer's Purple Tail," In The New Streets and Roads. Chicago: Scott, Foresman, 1958.

Elkin, Benjamin. *The Loudest Noise in the World.* New York: Viking Press, 1954.

Epstein, Samuel. *George Washington Carver.* Garrard Press, 1960.

Geisel, Theodore Seuss. *Horton Hatches the Egg.* New York: Random House, 1954.

———. *Horton Hears a Who.* New York: Random House, 1954.

———. *Thidwick, the Big-Hearted Moose.* New York: Random House, 1958.

Grantoff, Christian. *The Stubborn Donkey.* Adaddin Books, 1969.

Gudrum, Thorne-Thomsen. *The Giant Who Had No Heart in His Body. A Book of Giant Stories.* New York: Dodd, Mead & Co., 1926.

Moore, Lillian. *The Terrible Mr. Twitmeyer.* Eau Claire, WI: E.M. Hale & Co., 1952.

Steptoe, John. *Stevie.* New York: Harper & Row, 1969.

Voist, Judith. *Alexander & the Terrible, Horrible, No Good, Very Bad Day.* New York: Atheneum, 1977.

Zolotow, Charlotte. *The Quarreling Book.* New York: Harper & Row. 1963.